Handling

Life's Struggles

31 Daily Devotionals to Help You Understand, Navigate, and Appreciate Life's Various Struggles

Shawn M. McBride

Handling Life's Struggles

ISBN-13:

978-1986754071

ISBN-10:

1986754073

Printed in USA by 48HrBooks (www.48HrBooks.com)

Dedication

I want to sincerely dedicate this book to every adversity, trial, obstacle, setback, roadblock, hurdle, challenge, problem, tribulation, barrier, detour, rejection, blocked blessing, misfortune, difficulty, hardship, suffering, pain, and struggle that I have ever experienced in my life.

For it was each of you who really taught me and helped me reach this place and point in my life. What I have learned and gleaned from you has been life-changing and invaluable along this journey. You continue to be my teachers.

Table of Contents

Introduction

Once upon a time a young boy was playing outdoors in his backyard. He noticed a butterfly struggling to emerge from a small hole in a cocoon that was hanging on a tree branch. He could tell that the fuzzy creature was having a really difficult time getting out of the cocoon. As he watched this process with great anticipation for almost an hour, he became even more concerned with the plight of the butterfly. He could see the creature through the thin, silk-like material of the cocoon trying to break free, but he grew more and more impatient because it was taking so long. Even though the butterfly worked and worked, it didn't seem to be making much progress. The boy decided he would do something to help.

He found a small stick on the ground near the tree and used it to make the hole a little bit larger so that the butterfly would not have to struggle so much to come out. Soon after the butterfly emerged from the cocoon; however, it quickly fell straight to the ground below.

As the butterfly came out of the cocoon, the boy was surprised and astonished at what he observed next. It seemed very odd and confusing to him that the butterfly had an extremely swollen body and very small wings that were warped, wrinkled, and shriveled. He noticed that the winged creature was having even more difficulty attempting to get off the ground and into the air. After another twenty minutes of intense observation and bewilderment, the butterfly gave up trying and eventually spent the rest of its time crawling around on the ground as if it was still a caterpillar. It appeared it would never able to take flight.

The next day when the boy went to school, he told his science teacher about his experience and asked for an explanation. His teacher communicated to him that the butterfly was supposed to go through the struggle of emerging from the small hole. He shared with the boy that the struggle was absolutely necessary. He explained that the difficulty and adversity of squeezing through the small hole was so that the fluid in the center of the caterpillar's body would push out into the wings. This fluid was exactly what the butterfly needed to strengthen its wings to be able fly. The process allows the butterfly to develop its strength, determination, and resilience.

Even though the boy had good intentions in seeking to help the butterfly, he aborted the struggling process. Inadvertently, he hurt the butterfly's chances at a successful life

This amazing story is a simple reminder and powerful illustration of the importance of struggle. You see, without struggles in life we will never be able to soar and reach our full potential. Without struggle we cannot grow. Without struggle we cannot develop the capacity to live out our full purpose. As it is for the butterfly, so it is for every human being. Struggle is necessary to our development.

Sometimes struggles are exactly what we need in our lives to strengthen us. If God allowed us to go through life without any struggles, it would cripple us, just like the butterfly. We would never be able to fulfill our purpose.

Ultimately, we should be grateful for our struggles (hard as that may be). They are the events in life that give us wings and show us how strong we really are.

In fact, as Isabel Allende said, "We don't even know how strong we are until we are forced to bring that hidden strength forward. In times of tragedy, of war, of necessity, people do amazing things. The human capacity for survival and renewal is awesome."

Day 1: The Reality of Struggles

James 1:2 (NKJV) My brethren, count it all joy when you fall into various trials ...

I recently read a national survey that was conducted in which people all over America were polled and asked: "If you could ask God one question, what would it be?" The top response was, "Why is there pain and suffering in the world?" In other words people everywhere seem to be asking the age-old question: Why do bad things happen to good people?

I would like to suggest to you that struggles, problems, trials and bad things are not optional—they are inevitable and inescapable. Our introductory verse does not say "IF" you encounter bad things; it says WHEN you encounter them. It is not a matter of "IF" rather it is a matter of "WHEN." This reminds me of the Pinterest graphic that I saw that read: "Be kind, for everyone you meet is fighting a battle." The only sure way to exit struggles is to exit this life—and then who knows what lies ahead?

The truth of the matter is that, regardless of your age, race, location, and other demographics, you will face battles and struggles in your life. And you're not alone. Struggles do not care if you are young or old. They do not prefer men over women, the rich over the poor, or even sinners over saints. We all have struggles. We all have difficulties. We all have disappointments. It is just like your high school mid-term exams. No one is exempt.

As Sean Covey said, "Don't struggle about the struggle. In other words, life's full of ups and downs. So if you're struggling, don't worry, everyone else has or will at some point."

According to the introductory verse, James 1:2, the word "trials" is plural. This suggests that trials come in various forms. The word that is used here is "poikilos" and means colored or varied. It is the word for our English term "polka dot" or multicolored like a rainbow. The idea is that we are going to have all kinds of struggles; varied kinds, struggles of all stripes.

Friends, you are not alone! All over this planet, at this very moment, people are facing various trials.

The word "trials" is a term that also can broadly mean afflictions, adversities, difficulties, or life's struggles. There are physical, emotional, financial, family-related, and various multifaceted struggles that we all face. Someone loses a job for no apparent reason. A couple who was dating and or married just breaks up. Someone has an illness that has been lingering for a very long time and cannot seem to get it cured. A parent is grieving because of a wayward child. Someone experiences the sudden and tragic loss of a loved one. A young teenager no one believes in has to overcome the trials of the doubt and perhaps the mockery of his/her peers. The single mother seeking to raise two children alone has to overcome financial hardships. Elderly people have to deal with the trials of constantly thinking about mortality; the time they have left, and what to do with it even as they suffer the ills and pains of the aging body.

There was once a famous male movie star named Errol Flynn. He was an A-lister during Hollywood's Golden Era, widely known as a ladies' man. Of course, he was rich too, and famous. Seems to have had it all, didn't he? Yet Flynn once said that he had cried more than people would ever know.

There is no life so charmed that it is a stranger to struggle. In fact I've discovered that every single person in this world is in one of three categories:

1. About to face a trial

2. Already in a trial

3. Just coming out of a trial

Which one of these categories do you find yourself in today?

The good news is that, wherever you find yourself, you can still remain joyful. This is what I think James means when he says: count it all joy!

Of course, it's not natural or our first instinct to remain joyful when we are having trouble! Yet it is very crucial to understand that this is one of the keys to our growth. Learning to properly respond to adversity will make a huge difference in your life.

Anyone can count it all joy when everything is going their way and life is breezy. It's easy to smile when there are no problems in your life. What we need to learn is that instead of getting angry and mad in the midst of our trials and adversities, we should really become glad. Why? Because clearly the Lord is up to something in our lives.

Counting it all joy certainly does not mean that we pretend that we are not having problems or that we throw a party for our suffering. The phrase "count it" is a term that simply means "to evaluate." It is a term that is used by a CPA or a bank teller who is adding up numbers to make sure that the balance spreadsheet turns out right. When trouble comes we must evaluate our trials from the Lord's point of view, not necessarily from our human point of view.

One dissenter in the former Soviet Union was sent to a Siberian prison camp unjustly. Siberian winters get down to fifty and sixty degrees below zero. The Siberian "gulag" system of prisons was a freezing death camp experience. Yet the dissenter, Nobel Prize winner Alexander Solzhenitsyn, said that he was grateful for his prison experience. He said it *made* him; it re-created him into a man who could have a strong impact on the world for good.

When facing adversity, we must think ahead to how this experience can mold us into being stronger, greater people. That does not mean we should accept injustice. It does mean understanding that suffering is a great teacher --- perhaps the greatest teacher of all --- and that some suffering is inevitable in each of our lives.

As Shakespeare said, "Let me embrace thee, sour adversity, for wise men say it is the wisest course."

Questions for Consideration

1. What trial in your life can you honestly count for joy?

2. What did you learn from this trial?

3. Did you become stronger for the struggling?

Day 2: Life Lessons From Charlie Brown

Psalms 46:1 (NLT) God is our refuge and strength, always ready to help in times of trouble.

I grew up just outside of Washington, D.C. in the suburbs of Prince George's County, Maryland. One of my favorite childhood pastimes was getting the Sunday newspaper that was delivered to our home and looking at all of the comic strips. My all time, go to comic strip was *Peanuts,* written by Charles M. Schulz. This particular series focused on a group of young kids who all lived in the same neighborhood. Kids like Linus, Lucy, Peppermint Patty, Marcie, Schroeder, and, of course, the dog Snoopy kept me engaged with their various antics.

The main character in the story line was a little boy named Charlie Brown. What fascinated me about him and still does to this day was that he always—and I mean always—had some kind of struggle going on. He always seemed to have problems.

In one particular strip Charlie was building a beautiful sandcastle. He worked on it for several hours. After completion he took a step back, looked at it, and just as he was admiring it, a major storm came out of seemingly nowhere and blew over all of his sandcastle. He stood where his beautiful masterpiece was, on level sand, saying to himself, "I know there's a lesson in this, but I'm not sure what it is."

I will never forget Charlie and his female friend Lucy, with whom he would often play catch football as well as practice kicking the ball. Over and over again, whenever Charlie would run towards Lucy to kick the ball, as if he was trying to make a field goal or extra point, Lucy would always pull the ball away at the very last second (in spite of her promises not to do so!). As a result Charlie would land flat on his back.

Can you relate to Charlie's struggles? Can you picture your own sandcastles being blown away after much time and effort? Do you ever feel like you always get the short end of the stick, so to speak, no matter how hard you try? Is your good fortune always whisked away at the last moment?

I believe that in many ways we are all like Charlie Brown. The one thing we all have in common is that we have had unexpected struggles. Unanticipated storms come into our lives and wipe out our sandcastles. These storms leave us confused and bewildered. We are left looking around, trying to figure out exactly what happened and why it happened. We keep trying to accomplish a particular goal, and we put forth determination, effort, and energy only to discover the target continues to move further and further away form us.

Charlie Brown's life and various struggles reminds me of the opening verse:

Psalms 46:1 (NLT) God is our refuge and strength,

always ready to help in times of trouble.

You see, when the days seem dark and our struggles are great, we must always remember that God is still with us and loves us. We each have a purpose and a meaning that makes us special in God's eyes. I encourage you to always turn to Him so He can lead and guide you through your struggles.

Remember that you learned something building those sandcastles that are now in ruins. You picked up skills; you gained strengths; you learned how to engineer a sandcastle better than you knew before. If you pick up the pieces and start over again, turning to God in your struggle, then one of these days you'll build a sandcastle that no wind can destroy.

That will be because God will be by your side, strengthening and teaching you how to do it right.

When the Lord builds, the structure has staying power, and "unless the Lord builds the house, the builders labor in vain." (Psalm 127:1).

Questions for Consideration

1. What sandcastles—fond dreams—that you spent time and effort carefully building are lying at your feet in ruins today?

2. Are you ready to start building new ones—better, smarter, and stronger dreams—with the Lord by your side?

3. What football that you were all lined up to kick out of the park has been snatched away from you?

4. Is it possible you were trusting in human beings, not God, when that happened?

Day 3: Labor & Delivery

John16:21(NLT)
It will be like a woman suffering the pains of labor. When her child is born, her anguish gives way to joy because she has brought a new baby into the world.

I am the proud father of five amazing children. Children are truly a blessing from the Lord and His most precious creations. Everyone loves babies! When you see a cute baby, you can't keep your eyes off him or her. You may even be tempted to indulge in a little baby talk or to grab the little feet.

Yet despite all the cuteness, babies' arrivals are not always the most pleasant experiences. Whether you are a woman in labor or someone watching a woman in labor, it is apparent that labor does not feel like butterflies and tickles. Labor can be very painful; not only that, it can be long and tiring.

Here you are, carrying this baby for the longest nine months of your life, and it is finally time to birth this beautiful creation that has been growing on the inside of you. They have the room prepped for delivery, everything is ready, and all hands are on deck. This is the moment you have been waiting for. When it is time for the baby to come, there is no looking back. When a baby is ready to leave the womb, that is exit time, and there's no stopping it. You have to go through it until the delivery is complete, however long and hard that time period may be.

I don't know if you have ever had contractions or witnessed someone have them, but they are no fun. They keep coming, and they don't stop until the baby is born. Not only do they not stop; they get worse. They start becoming more frequent and stronger the closer you come to delivering the baby.

The beauty of labor and delivery is that once you lay eyes on that little bundle of life, everything that you went through becomes nonexistent. The morning sickness, the heartburn, the weight gain, the pain, is nothing to be compared with finally laying eyes on your precious child.

Each child is unique and has his or her own personality and distinctive features. It is for the delivery of that which we labor. It's like Ellen DeGeneres said: "It's our challenges and obstacles that give us layers of depth and make us interesting. Are they fun when they happen? No. But they are what make us unique. And that's what I know for sure... I think."

That little "I think" shows how some women feel about childbirth. There are women who swear they will never have children again due to their bad labor or pregnancy experiences. At the same time, when they see that baby, full of the layers of depth and the beauty of a child of God, it makes the struggle of labor worth it every time.

Many of us have been pregnant with the things of God, and we are starting to feel labor pains. I don't know about you, but I have been through a lot of difficult and painful circumstances in my life. I find that when you are coming into what God has for you, Satan starts to fight you. He doesn't want you to get what God has for you, to live the life that He has created you to live. So, he hits you with blow after blow like those pesky contractions. Man, are contractions frustrating, but they are also encouraging because the worse they get, the closer you are to delivery.

I remember being told a story by a friend of mine who had an important meeting to attend in California.

Satan did all that he could to stop her from going. The closer the time got for her to go, the harder he fought for her to stay.

Satan see's you pregnant with the things of God and he does not want you to deliver. What he is doing cannot stop the delivery of God's promises from coming to fruition in your life. I know the contractions don't feel good, and things may seem to be getting more painful, but you are only getting closer. There is no stopping you now. You have come too far now not to deliver.

Stay focused on God and be ready to push because you are going to give birth to all that He has for you. When it is all over, the hard times you went though will be nothing compared to the fulfilled promise and purpose of God coming to pass in your life.

Questions for Consideration

1. You have advanced this far in your life. Can you turn back now?

2. Can you bear the intensity of your pain for a short time longer?

3. Do you believe God has begun a good work in you and will finish it?

Day 4: Our Struggles Produce Endurance

James 1:3 (NIV)… because you know that the testing of your faith produces perseverance.

I honestly do not believe that while on this earth we will be able to fully understand and comprehend the various reasons that we face certain trials. Many people cry out: "Why, Lord, why?" Yet they feel that the answer doesn't come.

Our verse for today reminds us that God is truly up to something in our lives. James 1:3 gives us one interesting reason as to why we face struggles. This understanding of "why" a certain trial has come can truly make the difference between you being victorious over your trials versus your trials being victorious over you. Knowing "why" you are facing certain situations can impact you emotionally.

Almighty God allows struggles to come into our lives in order to produce something in us. He wants to produce perseverance or endurance. Why? So that we can be heroes of God!

As Christopher Reeve said after his life-changing accident: "A hero is an ordinary individual who finds the strength to persevere and endure in spite of overwhelming obstacles."

The word perseverance actually means endurance. It literally means "to remain under" or to "stay put" in a trial until its specific purpose has been accomplished.

A good example of this is what happens when a person undergoes surgery. In order for the patient to have health restored he or she must remain under the surgeon's anesthesia. The patient must stay put and remain under the surgeon's knife in order for the desired outcome to happen. Jumping off the table and running out of the operating room will only prolong the problem and make matters worse.

We should not run from problems; rather we should endure them so that our faith can grow and become stronger. You see, growth is what God desires to produce in us. God's desire for all of His children is spiritual maturity. Trials, suffering, and struggles ultimately test our faith. These difficulties are literally putting our faith on the witness stand and calling for testimony as to the validity of our faith.

It's easy to declare that we have faith in God when life is a breeze. However, the true test of faith is not when life is easy. It is when life is hard. Our faith is strengthened by testing.

There was a funny story about testing when a college student was taking a final exam in ornithology, the scientific study of birds. The professor administering the test had a reputation on campus as being a very tough teacher. As a result this student spent an enormous amount of time preparing for this test. The day of the test he went to the classroom feeling confident that he would ace it. To his surprise instead of having a normal test based on what he studied, there were fifteen pictures of birds' feet on the test paper. The purpose of the test was to identify the birds by their feet!

The student was livid and said to the professor, "This is ridiculous. I cannot take this test. This is not what I prepared for!" The professor responded, "You must take it." The student said, "I'm not going to. I refuse." The professor replied, "You have to take it, or you will fail the class." The student responded, "Go ahead and fail me. I'm not going to take this test." The professor said, "All right. That's it. You've failed. Tell me your name." The student rolled the jeans he was wearing all the way up to his ankles and said, "You tell me!"

Now, we can understand why this student was defiant. The test didn't seem fair; he'd already worked hard on the material he thought he was supposed to know. At the same time we can pretty much figure out that the professor eventually found out his name and gave him a failing mark.

Let's not be defiant and fail God's tests. When times get tough, it is time to strengthen our faith muscles.

I love how the Apostle Peter encouraged his audience as they were faced with many different tests and trials.

… In all this you greatly rejoice, though now for a little while you may have had to suffer grief in all kinds of trials. 7 These have come so that the proven genuineness of your faith—of greater worth than gold, which perishes even though refined by fire—may result in praise, glory and honor when Jesus Christ is revealed. 1 Peter 1:6-7 (NIV)

Questions for Consideration

1. Have you ever asked "Why, Lord, why?"

2. Is the development of endurance important to you?

3. Do you want to be a strong person?

4. What was the last test of faith you went through and passed?

Day 5: The Adversity Lesson of Milton, Mr. Hershey Chocolate

Proverbs 3:5-6 (NLT) Trust in the Lord with all your heart; do not depend on your own understanding. Seek his will in all you do, and he will show you which path to take.

One of my all-time favorite inspirational stories comes from the life of Milton Hershey, who invented the delicious, mouth-watering milk chocolate Hershey's candy bar and other incredible sweet treats. Hershey is someone who struggled mightily with many adversities in his life, but he never gave in to the temptation of failure. Finally, he became a giant success.

Hershey only had a fourth grade education by the age of twelve. He dropped out of elementary school (you could do that in those days) and began working as an apprentice for a printing company in Lancaster, PA. This was short-lived; he was terminated a few years later. After another four year apprenticeship for a small candy maker, he borrowed money from his close family and ventured out and started his first candy business in Philadelphia.

Despite working day and night six days per week, this new venture was extremely short-lived. Hershey eventually ran out of money and went bankrupt. He felt like a total and complete failure. He was depressed. Milton's father, who lived in Denver, asked Milton to come join him in a get-rich-quick scheme. He went, only to find that his father had just missed the silver rush and was also struggling and jobless. There was still a silver lining, though! Being in Denver allowed young Milton to meet a local Denver candy maker who taught him to add fresh milk to caramel candy. This would extend the shelf life. At the time this was a bit of a trade secret.

Hershey was inspired again used his excitement to push for new backing. He went to New York City, where he opened another candy business. Sadly the invested money ran out, causing that venture to fail too. His family was disappointed in him and referred to him as irresponsible, impractical, and a hopeless dreamer. He was forced to return home broken yet again.

Hershey had faith and persisted in the face of his struggles. He eventually found a good business partner, secured additional financing from another family member, and pushed a cart carrying his hand-made candies on the streets of Lancaster, selling them to local residents. One day an English candy merchant traveling through tasted Hershey's unique candy. This merchant was also a large importer. He instantly fell in love with the fresh taste of Hershey's candy. He placed a large order and The Lancaster Caramel Company was launched. Soon enough Hershey began making chocolate and cocoa products. The Hershey Chocolate Company that we know today became so wildly successful it survived two World Wars and the Great Depression.

Milton Hersey became rich, successful, and a kind-hearted, civic leader by the age of thirty-five. This was because, in the face of his struggles, obstacles, and challenges, he chose to have faith and carry on with his dreams. He believed in himself and his ideas. He never allowed hard times to keep him from pursuing his dreams.

One of the tremendous benefits of his financial success was establishing, along with his wife Catherine, the foundation of what is now called the The Milton Hershey School. For more than one hundred years now, Milton Hershey School has helped at risk, poor children to realize their full potential by offering them top-notch education and housing . In addition Hershey also was the visionary leader and founder of what we today know as Hershey Theme Park located in Hershey, PA.

Milton Hershey's life story teaches us that the path to success in life (however you define success) is always littered with roadblocks and challenges. Setbacks are inevitable as you journey towards whatever it is you are seeking to accomplish. There is never constant smooth sailing.

Sometimes in life you will find yourself taking two steps forward and four steps backwards. Hershey's story reminds us to continue to be resilient. He could have made the decision to give up immediately after the first candy business failed, but he did not. He could have given up after the second venture failed. Once again he did not. Instead of giving up he chose to keep pressing forward until he accomplished what he set out to do.

I'm so glad that he did. Now he is a great American icon we can all look up to as an example of someone who didn't let failure and setback put him down for the count. His victory is our victory too; let's take inspiration from his perseverance in the face of adversity.

Questions for Consideration

1. Do you think most people would have given up after the first bankruptcy?

2. How about the second?

3. What encouraging signs did Hershey find along the way that gave his career a boost? Do you think those were signs from God?

4. Have there been times when even your family questioned what you were doing and lost faith in you?

Day 6: Joseph—Trusting in God When Life Isn't Fair

1 Peter 5:6
Humble yourselves therefore under the mighty hand of God,
that He may exalt you in due time.

There were many people in the Bible who probably had the right to have a really bad attitude. Joseph was one of them. God had given Joseph an amazing and inspiring dream. In his excitement, he responded like many of us would. He told his family about his dream, except it wasn't just any dream. He dreamed his family would bow down to him and he would rule over them. Joseph was eventually sold into slavery out of jealousy by his brothers, who hated him for his dream, not to mention that he was their father's favorite. They couldn't stand the possibility that Joseph would one day rule over them.

After being sold into slavery, Joseph's new Egyptian master saw the Lord was with Joseph, and he made Joseph the overseer of his house. Joseph's master, Potiphar, didn't even have to know what was going on in his house because he entrusted all things into Joseph's hands. Yet Potiphar was not the only one who had taken notice of Joseph. So did the master's wife. She wanted Joseph to sleep with her. Fortunately, because he had integrity, he consistently refused.

This woman was so infuriated by his denial she concocted a false story and framed him for attempted rape. This was no small allegation, and his master did not take it lightly. As a result Joseph was thrown in jail for a crime he did not commit. While in prison he was again being treated unfairly. But the unfair treatment from those around Joseph couldn't stop God from favoring him. Even jail could not stop the blessing and the favor of the Lord that was on Joseph's life. The keeper of the prison made Joseph overseer of all the prisoners.

On another occasion Pharaoh, the ruler of Egypt, had a dream. The chief butler thought of Joseph, telling Pharaoh about Joseph's ability to interpret dreams. They called for Joseph, and he interpreted Pharaoh's dream.

The dream was one of famine and lack, but God gave Joseph a grand plan to keep food in the land. They needed a man to execute this plan, and what better man was there than Joseph himself? Pharaoh made Joseph a ruler over his house and over all the people of the land. There was no one in higher in rank than Joseph other than Pharaoh.

He was given the ring from Pharaoh's hand as a sign of his authority, fine linen to wear, and a gold chain was placed around his neck. He rode in Pharaoh's second chariot. In time his brothers came and bowed before him, begging for food as relief from the famine in their land.

Joseph's dream had become manifested before his very eyes, despite many struggles to get there. God was faithful to fulfill his dream and was there blessing him every step of the way.

In spite of all of these unfair adversities and trials, there weren't any complaints from Joseph or grumblings about how awful things had turned out for him. He stayed faithful to God and kept his eyes on the one who favored him. God was with Joseph every step of the way, so much so that those around him noticed the favor of God on his life.

Did you know that you are no different than Joseph? You too have God on your side, who is able to make all things abound toward you even in your times of struggle and trial, and even when things aren't fair.

As Maria Shriver said,"Everybody has tragedy in their life. Everybody has hurdles in their life. Everybody has tough things to overcome. My kids say to me, 'This isn't fair.' I said, 'Life isn't fair.'

Everybody has their issues. It's how you handle your issues that distinguishes you."

Even in unfortunate and unjust circumstance, Joseph realized that God had a purpose for him that was ultimately good . For Joseph, his life was not just a series of unrelated events. I honestly believe that in his heart Joseph realized that God was still in control and was eventually going to bring good out of his painful circumstances. I can conclude this because of what he said years later as he was having the conversation with his brothers when they were reunited by their need in the famine:

Genesis 50:20 (NLT) You intended to harm me, but God intended it all for good. He brought me to this position so I could save the lives of many people.

In spite of his struggles Joseph maintained personal integrity. When Potiphar's wife tried kept asking Joseph to sleep with her, he could have very easily given in to his flesh and the pressure to commit sexual sin. Instead he chose to do what was right. He chose the path of honor instead.

You must develop the strength of character that causes you to maintain your personal integrity when the pressure to do wrong is on. There was no compromise whatsoever with Joseph. He never once rationalized in a way that made it okay for him to make the wrong choice. We mustn't do that either.

In due time God exalted Joseph to exactly where he was supposed to be. There were certainly times when Joseph couldn't see that coming! Sometimes our life takes a different direction, or we take a wrong turn. Yet God is able to make sure we still get to our destination as long as we humble ourselves and trust Him.

Don't give up on your dreams just because there is some struggle involved in the process. God will take every detour and wrong turn you made and make sure you still get to the dream that He placed inside of you.

Don't fret. Be encouraged. No matter what the circumstances look like now, if you are faithful the Lord will exalt you in due time.

Questions for Consideration

1. Have detours and setbacks ever made you stop believing in your hopes and dreams?

2. Do you think Joseph went through moments of extreme discouragement in prison, thinking maybe God had deserted him?

3. Had God deserted Joseph?

4. Has God deserted you?

Day 7: Hakuna Matata—No Worries

Matthew 6:25-27; 33 (NLT) That is why I tell you not to worry about everyday life—whether you have enough food and drink, or enough clothes to wear. Isn't life more than food, and your body more than clothing? Look at the birds. They don't plant or harvest or store food in barns, for your heavenly Father feeds them. And aren't you far more valuable to him than they are? Can all your worries add a single moment to your life? Seek the Kingdom of God above all else, and live righteously, and he will give you everything you need.

Sitting at her desk waiting for the next call, Amanda received a message from one of her managers: "I would like you to meet me in my office at 1:00."

"Why in the world would the manager want me to meet her in the office?" she thought to herself. She immediately started to think of all the things she had done wrong that week: the times when she was late, when she may not have done everything perfectly on a phone call. Maybe there was even something she had done and forgotten about! Just in case there was, Amanda spent the next two hours thinking about what she could be getting in trouble for. So many people had been getting fired lately, Amanda just knew she was next.

It is funny how we can start to worry about something before we have even been given a reason to worry. It is like we run at the opportunity to worry about things.

The more Amanda worried about what this impromptu meeting was for, the slower time moved. She was tired of waiting and just wanted to get it over with. She even asked her neighbor for their guess as to what the meeting could be about.

"Do you think I'm in trouble?" she asked in fear.

"Just wait until you get in there and stop trying to figure it out," her coworker said. That was easier said than done.

Amanda's manager had never called her in the office before, so why now? Amanda worked herself into such a tizzy over the meeting that she started messing up all her phone calls. The anticipation of the meeting had her so anxious she could not focus on what she was supposed to be doing. Amanda stared at the clock as 12:59 turned into 1:00. As anxious as she was for the meeting, now she was nervous to go. She got up from her desk and slowly made her way to her manager's office.

"Come on in, Amanda," her manager said.

She sat down hesitantly, trying to brace herself for the news she was about to receive, wishing she would have updated her resume so she could look for a new job.

To her surprise Amanda spent the next twenty minutes in that office listening to her manager tell her what a good employee she was. Amanda was shocked to hear that her manager appreciated her hard work and that she had some of the best calls in all of the call center. By the end of the conversation, her manager had given her a raise and told her to keep up the good work. All Amanda's worrying was for nothing.

Why is it that our instinct is to worry? The only thing it changes is our stress level. When she heard about the meeting, why didn't Amanda automatically think that she was getting a raise or being praised for her good work?

Unless you have trained yourself to expect God's goodness and blessings in your life, you will struggle with worrying. Going through trials is bad enough without being concerned with every single detail, planning for the worst, and expecting that things are going to go badly.

Jesus taught us that we should take no thought for our life, that if we make him our focus and put him first he will add to us everything that we need. Jesus said in this same chapter that it is those who do not know him who worry about their provision and their needs. We should not be like the people of the world, wondering where our next meal is going to come from. (See Matthew 6:19-34.)

Are you worried about what is going to happen to you, worried about how you are going to make it through this tough time in your life? Take that same energy you're using to worry and seek God's kingdom. Find out what He says about your situation, and know that He will take care of everything you need as you put Him first.

He didn't say that some things would be added to you. He said all. When you fill your heart with God's Word, it leaves no room for worry. Seek God first and ditch the worries, because God will add all things unto you. Expect His goodness and blessings in your life.

Questions for Consideration

1. Have you ever worried about something that turned out well and you realized you had nothing to worry about?

2. Are you worried about something that is yet to happen or come?

3. Does worrying about things do any good?

4. What is an alternative to worry?

Day 8: No Pain No Gain

1 Timothy 4:8 (NLT) Physical training is good, but training for godliness is much better, promising benefits in this life and in the life to come.

At the time of this writing, I am on a ninety-day exercise journey. Today is day thirty-one. Working out and eating healthy can be difficult. It takes discipline and patience to see results. Eating healthy tends to be the more difficult part, at least for me. I don't know about you, but choosing a salad instead of a nice, juicy cheeseburger with hot seasoned fries can be downright painful for me. Without the healthy choices and the time spent in the gym, though, there will be no results. Without the pain of the process there is no gain.

Have you ever been lifting weights and got to the last set? The last set is the hardest one to lift. It is a struggle to pull the weight up, but it is the struggle that builds the muscle.

The struggle you are going through is also building your spiritual muscles. They are increasing your faith and developing character in you. Every time you face an obstacle in your life, you are lifting a weight. Going through it may be painful, but it is making you stronger. When you meet people who have been through a lot of things in life, they are usually the strongest people. You can put them up against anything, and they will not fold.

God is using your time of hardship to strengthen you, to prepare you for the next level of your life.

Yes, there will be times in our lives where we go through painful situations. God, being the loving father that He is, will turn that around for your good and use it to establish you on good ground. He will prepare you for the future things to come so that all that you have endured was not in vain or wasted. Jesus took on our pain so that we can gain everything he paid the price for. He never said it would be easy, but he has already done the hard part so that we can live life in abundance.

Exercise is great; it keeps you fit and healthy. Yet it will never be able to do for you what godliness can. It can never produce as many results in your life as your stance as a child of God. The Scripture says godliness has a promise that is for our life right now, here on earth, and for the life which is to come.

Many people live their lives going through trials in hope of the return of Christ because then all things will be made perfect. We will no longer have to endure the trials and tribulations of this world. Yet we do not have to wait until heaven, until the return of Christ to experience the goodness of God and the abundance in which we were called to walk.

Do not allow the situations in your life to become barriers for you. Let them instead be like weights that are lifted high, making you stronger, building your faith muscle, getting you fit to stand up against any situation that may come your way. Although your adversity may be the weight, Christ is the strength used to lift the weight and to keep lifting it until it is no longer heavy, until you have been made strong. So, don't give up. Keep lifting, keep getting stronger.

Questions for Consideration

1. Prayer, reading the Word, serving others, and watching our words are all spiritual exercises. Do you think they are harder or easier than physical exercises?

2. What can we learn about spiritual discipline when we think about and practice physical discipline?

3. Can you think of struggles as a way to build your faith muscle?

Day 9: P.U.S.H. Pray Until Something Happens

Luke 11:9-10 (NLT) And so I tell you, keep on asking, and you will receive what you ask for. Keep on seeking, and you will find. Keep on knocking, and the door will be opened to you. For everyone who asks, receives. Everyone who seeks, finds. And to everyone who knocks, the door will be opened.

There is a well-known story about a man who was awakened in his cabin one night by Jesus. The man was given instructions to push with all his strength against a giant boulder that sat in front of cabin. He was given no reason for this, nor the promise of a result. The man was simply told to "Push."

The next morning when the man arose, he went outside to do as he was told. Perhaps the instructions came to him in a dream, or perhaps Jesus actually appeared the previous night. Maybe the man imagined the entire scene, but something told him he needed to push, and so he did.

He pushed that entire first day from sunup to sundown. The boulder didn't budge. He set his shoulder against the cold stone until his body was weary, his mind was doubtful, and his heart was almost as heavy as that rock. Still, he went home, rested, and the next morning he went back out to try again. For weeks on end he pushed against the gigantic boulder. Each day the boulder stayed exactly the same and exactly where it was before. The man's heart was ever more doubtful, and his body was showing the effect of this painful task. Satan appeared to break the man's mind even further by tempting him into quitting. He told the man his task was impossible and that he was unworthy of the Lord's favor because his efforts were failing.

Sadly, the man began to believe those discouraging words and his efforts dwindled. He decided to put in minimum effort, which he did for awhile. One day he decided he couldn't live with either failing efforts or failing faith. He wanted answers.

It took three straight months, but he finally cried out to the Lord and said, "Lord, I have labored hard and long in Your service, putting forth all my strength and nothing is happening. I'm tired and failing. Why? What am I doing wrong???"

To the man's great surprise, the Lord replied with compassion.

"My friend, when long ago I asked you to serve Me and you accepted, I told you to push against the rock with all your strength and that you have done. But never once did I mention to you that I expected you to move it; at least not by yourself. Only I can move the boulder. Your task was to push. Now you come to Me thinking that you have failed and ready to quit. The opposite is true! Your arms are strong and muscled; your back sinewy and brown. Your hands are calloused and your calf muscles are muscular after pushing for three months. The muscles in your chest are swollen, and you have become emboldened and resilient. I was working on you and in you as you were pushing, even though you didn't realize it. Through opposition you have grown much, and your ability now far surpasses that which you used to have. Your calling was to be obedient and push, and to exercise your faith and trust in My wisdom, and this you have done."

The man had thought he was either foolish, unworthy or a failure. It turns out he was stronger and more credible, not only to himself but in the eyes of the Lord. He believed in himself more and his faith was strengthened. The man "prayed until something happened," and although it wasn't what he thought it would be, it was what he needed.

In the movie *Shadowlands*, C. S. Lewis (played by Anthony Hopkins) has married an intelligent fan of his Christian writings (played by Debra Winger). Unfortunately, it soon becomes evident that his new wife has cancer. When the cancer goes into remission, friends congratulate Lewis on how hard he has prayed. Lewis is not optimistic, though. He knows his wife's situation is serious. His comment is that prayer does not change God or His will. The only thing prayer has changed is Lewis himself.

Keep pushing that rock. It may never move. Yet you will be changed for the better; you will be stronger in facing your circumstances; and the contours of your big, new, beautiful faith muscles will appear in everything you think, say, and do.

Questions for Consideration

1. Is there a rock in your life that never seems to budge?

2. Have you found yourself growing in strength, faith, love, hope, and charity because you have pushed against it?

3. Is spiritual effort ever in vain, even if the results are different from what we anticipated?

4. Will you persevere in your path of faith?

Day 10: Daniel and the Lion's Den

Daniel 6:10 (NLT) But when Daniel learned that the law had been signed, he went home and knelt down as usual in his upstairs room, with its windows open toward Jerusalem. He prayed three times a day, just as he had always done, giving thanks to his God.

There was a decree made in the land that no petitions should be made to any man or God other than King Darius. Daniel, although aware of the new decree, continued to pray to God three times a day. His relentless devotion to God was against the signed decree of the king. People urged that he must pay the price, which was to be thrown into a den of lions. The king had respect for Daniel and tried his best to deliver him from being thrown into the den, but there was no way for him to overturn his own decree.

The king knew that God was with Daniel. He said, "The God who you serve continually will deliver you."

The mouth of the den was covered with a stone and sealed with the king's signet. There was no way for Daniel to escape his fate. The king was so worried about Daniel's fate, he stayed up all night fasting, unable to sleep.

The king arose first thing in the morning and hurried down to the lion's den.

"O' Daniel, servant of the living God, was your God who you serve continuously able to deliver you?"

God had sent an angel to shut the lion's mouth. There was no harm done to Daniel for he was found innocent before God and the king. The king ordered that Daniel be brought out of the lion's den. Due to his faith in God, there was not even a scratch on him.

Those who condemned Daniel took his spot in the lion's den. Not only they went in, but their whole families were condemned to this fate. The lions and the angels were not as gracious this time around. The people's bones were found lying in the bottom of the den. Then there was a new decree made by King Darius: everyone would tremble with fear before the God of Daniel.

Scripture Focus: Ephesians 6:18

Praying always with prayer and supplication in the Spirit and watching there unto with perseverance and supplication for all saints.

Despite the decree made to ensnare Daniel, he continued to keep God as the head of his life, praying three times a day. In the time of trial, David's response was to continue to seek God in prayer. I have no doubt that it was Daniel's prayer life that contributed to the trust he had in God. It not only caused his own deliverance but stirred the faith of the king, who went on to command all to worship the one and only true God.

Our prayer lives are vital to our relationship with God and victory over our struggles. You may not be thrown into a lion's den, but you may be thrown into a bad situation. Just as God closed the mouth of the lions for David, He will also come to your rescue. Daniel could have been stricken with fear, or counted his life as lost, but he didn't. He instead remained consistent in seeking God and refused to sacrifice his prayer life.

We all lead such busy lives. While trying to fit everything into our already tight schedules, it is usually our relationship with God that ends up getting sacrificed. Yet we cannot afford to neglect our private time with God. That is where we receive the strength and wisdom to be able to make it through the tough times. Don't allow yourself to get so overwhelmed with your problems or your schedule that you stop praying.

Scripture says to pray always. When we decide that praying is not important enough to have priority in our day, we are only doing ourselves a disservice. Continue to pray and develop a deeper relationship with God.

Daniel knew that the same God he prayed to three times a day, the one whom he refused to stop praying to, would deliver him. There was no escaping, no way out for him. The stone was rolled over the mouth of the cave, but still he had faith in God's deliverance.

Maybe they closed the door on your position at work. Maybe someone rolled the stone over to block your dreams, saying there is no way through for you. They counted you out, and you may have even counted yourself out. Yet take a lesson from Daniel and count God in. Spend time in prayer and never forsake your relationship and prayer life with God.

Questions for Consideration

1. Do you believe that God is a very present help in trouble?

2. Has God ever delivered you and yours from a "lion's den" of some sort?

3. Do you believe He will deliver you again?

Day 11: Hope in the Midst of Life's Hurdles

Isaiah 40:31 (NLT) But those who trust in the Lord will find new strength. They will soar high on wings like eagles. They will run and not grow weary. They will walk and not faint.

When I was in high school I competed in indoor/outdoor track as well as cross country running. One of the events that I could never muster up the courage to learn and compete in was hurdles. It always seemed so hard to run at full speed and jump over those things.

Have you ever jumped over a hurdle? The thing about jumping a hurdle is that you must build up momentum before you are able to make the jump. If you are not running with enough speed and jumping with enough height you are not going to make it. You may even hurt yourself.

Some of us are facing hurdles in our personal lives and trying to take them on without the momentum that is necessary.

We can experience setbacks in life that slow us down and try to make us stagnant. Satan is hoping they will decapitate us, so we are not able to move forward into the things that God has for us. Yet there is nothing big or small in this life that can stop us unless we allow it to. We like to talk as if life has the ability to stop us, but that is only because we are not fully aware of who and whose we are.

Hurdles are not obstacles for God. They are only Satan's tactic to slow you down, which is all he can do since he cannot stop you. We see the hurdles and get intimidated. "That hurdle is so high, I am just not sure if I can get over it," we tell ourselves. If you are trying to jump over the hurdle by yourself, then you are probably right. But when you allow

God to come in and be the help you need, the hurdle becomes nothing more than a stepping stone that God turns into something that sets you up for success for your next stage of life.

How do you build up momentum to jump over the hurdles?

The way you make it over the hurdle is by waiting on God. We always think we know what is best. Even when we don't know what is best, we will waste no time trying to figure it out and often fail in the process. We are in such a race against the clock, we feel like we don't have the time to wait for His help. God does not want you to try and figure things out for yourselves. Adam and Eve thought they had it all figured out and we see how well that went.

Adam and Eve did not have to take Satan at his word when he said they would be like God if they would eat the forbidden fruit. God was easily accessible to them. They could have gone to Him, telling him what happened, seeking His truth. You know what God would have said? "He is just trying to deceive you; you are already made in My image. That fruit is not going to bring you wisdom or life, but only death as I have already told you."

Yet we don't choose to seek God and His ways first, and when we don't, we give Satan an opportunity to come in and create challenges. We would much rather seek the ways of others, of Google, of YouTube, or anyone else that has some type of advice for us.

We need to bring the advice of others before God. Open your Bible and see if the advice of others lines up with the wisdom of His Word. If the answer is no, then it should not be heeded. He is the only one who knows what is right and what needs to be done. He is the only one who holds the master plan for your life. Why waste time going to other places, searching for others, when we can go straight to the source?

Don't allow other things to slow you down. Go straight to God so you can get the momentum that you need to jump over the hurdles in your life.

Questions for Consideration

1. What are some of the hurdles you are facing in your life right now?

2. Have you given yourself the momentum of turning to God?

3. How many hours per week do you spend surfing the Internet rather than seeking the source of all wisdom? Can you change the balance a bit?

Day 12: Through the Fire

Hebrews 13:5 (NLT) I will never fail you.
I will never abandon you…

To say that King Nebuchadnezzar was a confident man would be an understatement. He had a golden statue constructed in his image! As if that wasn't enough, when the music played everyone was to bow down and worship the statue. Soon he made a decree that whomever refused to bow when the music was played would be thrown into a fiery furnace. Everyone bowed down in worship to the statue.

Well, not everyone. Shadrach, Meshach, and Abed-nego did not bow to the statue nor serve the gods of the king. He was not pleased.

In fact, the king was enraged and commanded that the three Hebrew boys be brought before him.

"Is it true that you don't serve my gods and won't worship my image?" He told them that when the music played, they needed to fall down and worship his image. If not they would find themselves in a fiery furnace. He even mocked them by saying, "Who is the God that shall deliver you out of my hands?"

The response of the three Hebrew boys was one of courage and unshakeable faith.

"It is not necessary for us to answer you. If it be so our God whom we serve is able to deliver us from the fiery furnace and he will deliver us out of your hands. If not, just know that we will not serve your gods or worship your golden image."

The king was infuriated, and he commanded that the oven be turned up seven times hotter. Then the mightiest men in his army bound the three Hebrew boys and threw them into the fire.

The flame was so hot it slew those who were throwing them in the fire. The three Hebrew boys fell down, bound, into the midst of the fire. The king was astonished that they were not been burned to death

"Did we not cast the three men bound in the midst of the fire?" he asked.

They answered him, stating, "I see four men loose, walking in the midst of the fire, and they are not hurt. The fourth one is like the son of God."

The king then came near to the fire and said, "Shadrach, Meshach, and Abed-nego, you servants of the most high God, come forth."

They came out of the fire, and all who watched saw that the fire had no power over the three Hebrew boys. Not even their hair or clothes were burned. They did not even have the scent of fire on them.

There was a new decree made that anyone who would speak against the God of Shadrach, Meshach, and Abed-nego, would be cut into pieces.

The king declared "There is no other God that can deliver in this way."

Talk about a struggle! Their faith was in question, and they were in no way about to abandon their beliefs, not even for a moment. You too must have the same response when your life is under fire. You cannot abandon your belief in God's ability to save and His faithfulness. When we go through the trials and tribulations of life, we are never alone. Jesus was right there in the midst of the fire with the three Hebrew boys, and he is right there with you in your fire.

I know sometimes life is so loud you feel you cannot hear the voice of God and at other times it is so dark it seems that you cannot see his light. Regardless of how you feel, the truth is that God is right there with you. He has never left you and He never will. God is not scared of the fires in your life. You serve a God who is fire proof and who will bring you out of your hard times without even the scent of smoke. Just as with the three Hebrew boys, those around you will be amazed to see how God kept you during your troubles. When you are struggling, rest assured that God is right there with you. If he is there, then you know that He will bring you out. He is your ever present help in times of need.

Questions for Consideration

1. Have you ever been in a situation so tough, it felt like you were inside of a hot furnace?

2. Did your faith allow you to emerge unscathed?

3. Do you believe God will be at your side throughout all your struggles?

Day 13: Pressure Makes Diamonds

Zechariah 13:9 I will bring that group through the fire and make them pure. I will refine them like silver and purify them like gold. They will call on my name, and I will answer them. I will say, "These are my people," and they will say, "The Lord is our God."

Sometimes life can feel as though it is closing in on you. It is like you are in a room where the walls are closing in and the ceiling is coming down. Everywhere you look is another obstacle pressing in on you. You feel like your back is up against the wall with nowhere to go.

That's the pressures of life at times. Yet did you know that diamonds are made under pressure? The pressures of life are refining us. Like a diamond, when you come out on the other side of your high-pressure situations, you will be shining in the glory of God.

The pressures in your life will end up bringing out the best in you. While you are going through the struggle, it does not feel like you are being refined into your best self. Yet our feelings have way more influence over us than they should. Our emotions are supposed be subject to us, not the other way around. Don't let your emotions dictate your ability to overcome and be everything that God has called you to be.

When you refine something, you are removing the impurities from it. God is removing the impure things from your life. He is removing the things that He did not plant. There are weeds growing that are hindering your growth. While you are going though your trials, He will use that time to uproot those weeds.

The pressure is producing something in you that could not have been produced any other way. It is producing something in you that you are not yet able to see but that soon everyone will recognize. Now, everyone wants a diamond, but no one wants the pressure. When people see celebrities, or someone who has a lot of money, they become envious, not realizing what the people had to go through to have what now looks so effortless and luxurious. They had to sustain a lot of pressures.

The pressures that were meant to destroy you are used by God to make a diamond out of your hard times. We let them destroy us when we give in and decide not to fight anymore. But we should be willing to stand and fight. That is how He gets the glory that He so deserves. He takes what looked like something that should have defeated you, should have killed you, and brings you out of it without a scratch.

When you are going through adversity, think about the diamond: how beautiful it is, how much it shines in the light. That will be you when God is finished. Don't call it quits yet.

Don't worry about the pressures you face. They only mean that God is trying to make a diamond out of you.

Questions for Consideration

1. Are you a person who works well under pressure or one who doesn't?

2. Have you ever done something worthwhile because you were pressured to do so and were grateful that someone or something pressured you into doing it?

3. Have you ever thought of pressure as a process of refining for your soul?

Day 14: Defeating Your Giants

1 Samuel 17:45 (NLT) Then David said to the Philistine, "You come to me with a sword and spears. But I come to you in the name of the Lord of All, the God of the armies of Israel, Whom you have stood against. 46 This day the Lord will give you into my hands.

The Philistines and Israelites were staging for battle. There was a champion of the Philistines named Goliath, who stood almost ten feet tall. He had top notch armor, and it was no wonder why he was the champion. Goliath stood and cried out to the Israelite army: "Am I not a Philistine and are you not servants of Saul? Choose a man for yourselves and let him come down to me. If he is able to fight with me and kill me, then we will be your servants; but if I prevail against him and kill him, then you shall be our servants."

Saul and all of Israel were overcome with fear at the challenge of Goliath. No one was brave enough to step up and fight him. Goliath presented himself every day and night for forty days, but there was still no man who would battle him.

David's brothers were out with Saul and the other Israelites, cowering in fear of Goliath. David's father sent him out to bring food to his brothers. While David was doing so, Goliath came and spoke to the Israelites. When he did all the men fled. David was offended that Goliath would defy the armies of the living God.

Word got to Saul that David wanted to fight Goliath, and Saul requested that David meet him. Saul didn't think David was qualified to fight Goliath. David was young, and Goliath had been fighting all his life. David didn't care about any of that. He had kept his father's sheep and killed a lion and a bear trying to protect his father's flock. In his eyes this giant Philistine was no different.

Saul prepared David for battle by putting his armor on him. David had not tested the armor or used it before, so he took it off and went out to fight Goliath with only his slingshot and three stones.

When Goliath laid eyes on David, he was not impressed, and David was also not impressed or fearful of Goliath.

"You come to me with a sword and a spear, for the battle is the Lord's and he will give you into our hands," said David. Now that is what you call confidence. David ran towards Goliath, slung his stone and smote the Philistine on his forehead, who then fell flat on his face. David cut off his head for all to see, and the Philistines fled in fear.

Scripture Focus: Ephesians 6:13-17

Wherefore take unto you the full armor of God, so that you will be able to resist in the evil day, and having done everything, to stand firm. Stand therefore, having your loins girt about with truth, and having on the breastplate of righteousness; and your feet shod with preparation of the gospel of peace; Above all taking the shield of faith, wherewith ye shall be able to quench all the fiery darts of the wicked. And take the helmet of salvation, and the sword of the Spirit, which is the word of God.

When you are struggling to fight a battle that looks bigger than you, never trade in what God has given you for what he has given someone else. What God has for you is indeed for you. It gets easy to give up on your dreams as you go through adversity, but as a Christian you were created to be victorious. Just like David you must take off the armor of doubt and replace it with the full armor of God.

God has already equipped you with everything you need to overcome any circumstance that will try to come against you. Trust that what God has deposited in you is enough. Those around you may be trying to help by offering their advice and ill-fitting armor, but God has something better for you. He will fight your battles. Nothing can compare to having the almighty God fighting your battles for you.

Have confidence when you come against the giant circumstances in your life. When you make sure you are armed with the armor of the Lord, there is nothing in the world that can come against you and prevail. You are armed and ready for any battle. Those around you may doubt your ability to overcome, but as long as you are confident in God's ability, you will always come out on the other side a winner.

Questions for Consideration

1. Have you ever fought a giant problem?

2. Did you come out the winner?

3. Did God help you?

4. Could you have done it without God's help?

Day 15: Caleb and Joshua

2 Corinthians 5:7 (NLT) For we live by believing and not by seeing.

The promised land, a land flowing with milk and honey, was promised to the Israelites, the people of God. The Israelites spent forty years walking around in circles, trying to get there. Then they finally arrived, and the promised land was awaiting them on the other side. Yet although the land was promised to them, it was still occupied.

God commanded Moses to send out spies into the land to see exactly what their new home would look like and whether those who dwelled there were weak or strong. Among those spies were Caleb and Joshua. All the spies went into the same land, but not all the spies saw the same thing. After the spies searched out the land they came back and gave reports of what they had found.

They said the land was flowing with milk and honey just as God had promised. Yet they said the people in the land were strong for the people of God. At least that is what they implied.

Caleb wasn't fond of that report, which was rooted in fear. Instead he had something of his own to say: "Let us go up at once and possess it; for we are well able to overcome it."

How was Caleb able to see victory while everyone else saw defeat?

There were more spies that came with an even more fearful report: "The land that we spied out devours its inhabitants and all the men that we saw are of great stature. We saw giants of the son of Anak and we were as grasshoppers in their sight."

This report from the spies was enough to fill the whole congregation with fear. The promised land that they had spent years to reach, losing family members along the way of trying to obtain it, looked like it wasn't going to be a promise fulfilled after all.

The people cried and complained all night, feeling they had been led out of the land of Egypt for nothing. They even considered going back to Egypt after all they had been through.

Have you ever felt like turning back—like all of your faith and hard work was for nothing? It is a defeated feeling that leads many to give up and fall short of the promises of God.

Joshua and Caleb had enough of the fear-filled talk and plans for returning to bondage.

"The land that we passed through is very good land," they said. "If the Lord delights in us, then he will bring us into this land and give it to us. Don't rebel against the Lord or fear the people of the land; for they are bread for us, their defense has left them, and the Lord is with us: don't be afraid of them."

What do you see when you look at your own promised land? Are you seeing through eyes of faith or are you seeing through eyes of doubt? Maybe you don't consider it doubting because it looks like "reality". If you are trusting what you see with your eyes more than you are trusting the Word of God, though, that is unbelief.

It was because of the unbelief and murmuring of the Israelites that they were not able to enter the promised land. But guess who entered it? Yep. That's right: Caleb and Joshua.

I'm sure we have all heard the saying that perception is reality. That is true, and it is exactly what happened in this story. Some of the spies perceived that the men of the promised land were bigger and stronger than they were. Caleb and Joshua didn't care how big or strong they were. They knew that God had promised them the land, and if He said it was theirs, then He would make sure they were able to possess it.

What do you have your eyes on? The promises of God or the size of your circumstances? As long as your eyes are on your circumstances, they will always seem daunting. When you keep your eyes on the Word of God, though, He will show Himself to be bigger than your circumstances.

Are you struggling with something that seems larger than life, larger than God? Then you must put that obstacle in its place, which is under the feet of Christ.

The promises of God can be trusted and depended on. When you are standing on a promise of God, do not let what you see cause doubt. Instead, declare the promises of God and then watch them come to pass in your life.

Questions for Consideration

1. What things of promise seem to have slipped out of your reach?

2. Are you sure they cannot and will not come true?

3. How much fear is clouding your vision?

4. Can you look at your circumstances with faith not fear?

Day 16: The Struggles of the Baby Giraffe

2 Corinthians 4:8-12 (NLT) We are pressed on every side by troubles, but we are not crushed. We are perplexed, but not driven to despair. 9 We are hunted down, but never abandoned by God. We get knocked down, but we are not destroyed. 10 Through suffering, our bodies continue to share in the death of Jesus so that the life of Jesus may also be seen in our bodies

The life course of a baby giraffe is an amazing story that begins with fear and pain but ends with strength and success. From the instant a giraffe is born, its life is a struggle for survival and understanding; a front row seat to a horror show performed by none other than the newborn's mother.

The first thing a baby giraffe does is fall eight to ten feet to the ground, straight out of its mother's womb. Flooded with light and confusion, too weak to even move, the baby just curls into a ball and lies still.

The mother giraffe's first parental move is not so bad. It compassionately lowers its neck to kiss its new offspring. However, this first kiss really sets up a wildlife version of the sucker-punch, because the next thing the mother giraffe does is kick the baby so hard it flies up in the air and crashes back down on the ground, even more startled and confused than it already was. The baby's natural response is to curl up again, and the mother's natural response is to kick it again, over and over and over, until the first lesson is learned: Get up.

Trembling and still tired, the baby struggles to use its muscles and legs for the first time in an attempt to stop the kicking. The mother allows the baby to succeed, but instead of congratulating it, she walks over and – you guessed it – kicks it again.

This time, after falling from the forceful blow, the baby gets up quickly and stands upright with significantly less effort. Finally, the mother lets up and ends the violent process.

The struggle the newborn giraffe goes through is nothing short of monumental. There's a reason behind the mother's actions, however, and it's a reason we could all benefit from comprehending. The mother simply wants her baby to remember how—and why—it got up.

As human beings we are often born surrounded by doctors, nurses, and people who obviously love us. We enter the world in the hands of someone who makes sure we're safe and healthy. This does not happen in the world of giraffes, but there are good reasons for this.

Human beings have more comforts than do wild animals. We don't have lions, tigers, and hyenas stalking us every day, hoping to snag us as their meals. If the baby giraffe doesn't learn to get up and move quickly, it will not be long in the wild before it is devoured as food or literally "tripped up" and destroyed by weak moves.

What would be the human equivalent of this experience? How do we, as people, get "tripped up?" In truth we are under attack every day, either from other humans or by sin itself. What do we do to stand back up when life inevitably kicks and knocks us down? Are we thankful for the experience because it means we will learn, like the baby giraffe, to get up on our feet quickly and stay up?

Nature is sometimes cruel to be kind. A curled up baby giraffe is an edible target. It must be taught to stand. When life seems cruel, it is sometimes being kind to us. It is teaching us to get on our feet, put up our fists, and fight for our spiritual survival. Spiritually, let's face it: it's a jungle out there. Let's be thankful when we get knocked down, because it's an exercise in getting strong enough to stand up and fight.

Michelle Obama said, "You should never view your challenges as a disadvantage. Instead, it's important for you to understand that your experience facing and overcoming adversity is actually one of your biggest advantages."

Questions for Consideration

1. Have you ever felt cornered and then found the will to fight—for your dreams, for your marriage, for your children, or for your own well-being?

2. Wouldn't we be foolish to curl up and lie down in the spiritual jungle we face?

3. The next time you get knocked down by life, can you say, "Thank you" and get right back up?

Day 17: Your Will Be Done

Luke 22:42 (NLT) Father, if you are willing, please take this cup of suffering away from me. Yet I want your will to be done, not mine.

No one in the world has suffered through struggles like Jesus had. Yes, I am sure there have been people who have been beaten and hung, tortured and tormented. Yet Jesus was marred more than any man. At the end he felt forsaken by God, and he was carrying all the sins and sickness of the world in his body. His friends turned their backs on him; God Himself even turned His back on him for our sakes. Men, who were made in the image of Christ, rejected the very image of themselves.

Many believe that since Jesus was all man but still fully God, that he had no problem enduring the cross and enduring the trials and tribulations that were necessary to restore the children of God back to their Father. That isn't true.

Jesus himself had an inner struggle with not wanting to go through what needed to be done to save the world. We know that he prayed for the cup of suffering to pass from him (Luke 22:42 NIV) if that was at all possible. In Luke 22:44 NIV, it says that Jesus sweat blood as he prayed in the Garden of Gethsemane. This can actually happen. The National Institutes of Health say that under extreme stress, a person can suffer a condition called hematohidrosis. The blood vessels around the sweat glands constrict; then they swell and burst, and blood gets into the sweat. A person has to be under enormous mental anguish for this condition to occur.

We know that Jesus did not find the prospect of being whipped, beaten, mocked, crucified, speared, and otherwise tormented easy to face. No one would. He probably wanted to live on in order to do more good on this earth. Yet his desire to do God's will was greater than anything else. Throughout Jesus' whole life, his number one focus was fulfilling the will of God. He only said what he heard the Father say and he only did what he saw the Father do. He was in perfect alignment with the will of God.

It is easy to walk in obedience to the will of God when He wants you to heal people and do miracles or share the message of the gospel. The desire to fulfill the will of God is not so great when it means to be forsaken, beaten and tormented, and die a death of hideous agony, with nails hammered into your wrists and being unable to breathe from the pressure of being suspended by your arms on a cross. Even for the sake of all of humankind, that had to have been hard to face.

Is being obedient to the will of God worth if it includes struggles? Jesus thought so. If Jesus had decided that God's plan for his life was too difficult for him, none of us would have forgiveness of our sins or be able to have an intimate relationship with the Father.

In this life there will always be struggles, but you cannot let difficult times stop you from completing God's will for your life. The struggles we go through are nothing to be compared to the goodness that comes from them.

Walking in obedience doesn't always feel good, but it is always necessary. There is a grand plan for your life, and for that plan to come to pass you need to be obedient to God's will even when you don't feel like it, and even when it is hard.

The closer you get to God and the more you develop a relationship with Him, the easier it will be to live a life desiring that His will be done. When you don't know what the will of God is for your life, of course, it makes it difficult for you to desire it. If you want to know what the will of God is for you, you should look into the Word. The Bible is full of the knowledge of God's will for your finances, your marriage, your children, and for every area of your life.

If Jesus could fulfill God's will under such cruel and harsh circumstances, then you too can live to accomplish the will of God. Jesus said that we can do everything he did and even more (John 14:12). That means we can walk in the will of God successfully, just as Jesus did. So, when you go through struggles while fulfilling the will of God, let Jesus be your example and know that you can do all things through Christ who strengthens you.

Questions for Consideration

1. When you think of Jesus' struggles, do yours seem small by comparison?

2. Do you think Jesus was a man of tremendous courage?

3. Where did Jesus' strength come from?

4. Where should yours come from?

Day 18: I Think I Can

Proverbs 23:7 (KJV) For as he thinketh in his heart, so is he…

When I was little I remember reading the story of "The Little Engine that Could." You still hear this story being told today. Its purpose is to encourage children that they can do anything they put their minds to.

I thought it was just a story then, but I now know what the little engine was doing is actually founded in biblical truth. There is power in positive thinking. That is what the writer of the book was trying to convey.

This is very important. As Pat Riley said, "If you have a positive attitude and constantly strive to give your best effort, eventually you will overcome your immediate problems and find you are ready for greater challenges."

Briefly, the story of the little engine goes that there was a train riding along the tracks, carrying food, toys, and dolls for the kids who lived in a village. Running out of coal, the train broke down and someone had to help her get the food and toys to the children. There was a golden train that came riding by, and the toys stopped the train, hoping to get some assistance. The train was a passenger engine that only transported the best of people. The golden train would not help by pulling some broken down engine.

Then another train came riding by. It was a big strong engine that could easily pull the helpless train to the village. Yet that train claimed it only pulled freight cars full of important things. He had already finished work for the day and was tired. He declined to help the engine.

It seemed like there was no hope for the train until another engine was spotted. It was a little blue engine, the smallest of them all. She had never ridden over the mountain and knew it was going to be difficult. She wanted to help, though, and she wasn't going to let that hill stop her because she thought she could do it.

She began pulling the train saying, "I think I can, I think I can, I think I can." She continued to move up the hill faster and faster until she got the train to the village. She looked back over her triumph and said, "I thought I could, I thought I could!"

We can take away two lessons from this story. The first lesson is that you have to think you will make it over your hill. Some may call it thinking positively, but I call it thinking like God. It doesn't matter how steep the hill is or how heavy the load you are carrying. You must think that you can make it over the hill and get to the top.

What you think in your heart is what will be. That is why it is vital to align your heart with the heart of God through His Word. Align your heart with Scriptures like:

- No weapon formed against me shall prosper (Isaiah 54:17)

- Greater is he that is in me than he that is in the world (1 John 4:4)

- I am more than a conqueror in Christ (Romans 8:37)

- I can do all things through Christ who strengthens me (Philippians 4:13)

That is when you begin to move farther away from the struggle and closer to the victory.

Don't worry about the steep hill that is up ahead. Your current struggles are no surprise to God. People have been struggling with similar things throughout history. What's more, He has already planned an escape for you. You just have to believe it for yourself.

More important than thinking that you can, you must think that He can. You must believe that God is faithful and will deliver you from your present circumstances. Once you trust that He can, you will know that you can. God will empower and strengthen you to make it through any trial and tribulation. Just like the little engine, you will look back and say, "I thought I could." Then the next time you find yourself struggling up a steep hill, you will know exactly what to think and you will keep steaming along.

The second lesson that we take away from this story is that, unlike the train, we always have a present help. You don't have to worry about people who don't want to stop and help you or others who think you just aren't good enough. There is a helper who is always ready and waiting to come to your aid. You don't have to worry about whether He can help you make it up the hill or not. God is able to get you through any and everything that would try to stall your life.

Think you can, because even if you can't do it on your own power, there is Someone who can; Someone who is all-powerful and greater than any hills you are facing.

Questions for Consideration

1. What situation or situations have you conquered by thinking: "I can"?

2. Have you ever been able to do something you thought you couldn't?

3. Have you ever found that you had more strength than you thought you had?

Day 19: I Will Trust Him

Job 13:15 Job 13:15 (NIV)
Though he slay me, yet will I hope in him ...

Job was a man that had everything. He was prosperous and had a big, happy family. He was the greatest man of all the men in the east. Also, he was considered perfect and upright in the eyes of God. Job had it all!

God thought so highly of Job that He even shared His delight with Satan: "Have you considered my servant Job, that there is none like him in the earth, a perfect and an upright man, one that fears God and abstains evil?"

But Satan wasn't impressed. He asked, "Does Job fear you for no reason, have you not put a hedge around him, around his house and all that he has on every side? You have blessed the work of his hand and his substance has increased in the land, but if you put forth your hand and touch all that he has, he will curse you to your face."

God and Satan made a little bet. Everything Job had was put in the power of Satan, except Satan could not touch Job himself.

Satan set out to prove that Job would curse God if he did not have all the blessings and protection that God had given him. All of Job's children were killed; he also lost his livestock and his servants. Just when he thought things couldn't get any worse, Job was struck with boils from the top of his head to the soles of his feet. His wife even told him to curse God and die.

He was going through a tough time. Job had three friends come over who had supposedly come by to offer Job comfort and wisdom. Some friends! They insisted that Job must be guilty of some sin in order to suffer all of the loss and devastation that he was suffering. They certainly did not make things any better.

Job had no idea that Satan was the one behind everything that took place in his life. He thought it was God who was striking him, and he was feeling down and depressed, wishing he had never been born.

He was overwhelmed by the darkness in his life, but it was not enough to turn Job from God. Job had made up in his mind that regardless of what God had done to him, he would still trust Him. He refused to speak ill of Him.

What about you? Can you say that no matter what happens in your life, you will still trust God? If you get fired, if a loved one dies, if you start having problems in your finances, will you still trust God? Job was not the last person to blame his struggles on God. We are still blaming God for our troubles today. Every good and perfect gift comes from God; His plans of goodness for us should not be confused with Satan's plans to steal, kill, and destroy.

Although God is not the cause of the chaos, He will bring you out of it if you will choose to trust him like Job did. Trusting God is not something that just happens; it is a decision you must make within yourself. Regardless of what happens, you must trust that God is for you and not against you. Get rid of all the negative Nancys that are around you, only stating the obvious that is happening in your life. Put your trust in the one who is able to work all things for your good.

Do you know why I love the story of Job? Because after the struggle was over, God blessed Job with more than he had to begin with, twice as much to be exact. He restored everything that Job had lost, from his children to his cattle.

Has calamity all of sudden struck your life? Was all going well and then everything in your life started to take a turn for the worse? Have you lost everything?

God doesn't just have restoration for Job; He also has restoration for you. God is a God of restoration, and He will make your latter greater than your former. Don't give up now. Dig your heels into the ground and decide that you will trust God through the good times and the bad.

Job could have given up and taken the advice of his wife to curse God and die. Yet God had a track record with Job. Job was a blessed man prior to all his struggles and he was fully aware that God was the source of the goodness in his life. That is why he was able to trust Him.

God has a track record with you too. I bet if you took a few minutes, you could think of the different times when God came through for you, when He blessed you, when His grace showed up on the scene and caused things to work in your favor.

When troubles come in your life, take a moment and think on those things. Watch your trust in God rise as you remember His faithfulness to you in the past. He is the same God, and He is just as willing and able to be there for you now as He was then.

Questions for Consideration

1. When has God come through for you in the past?

2. What blessings has God bestowed on you?

3. Do you believe God wants to restore all that has been lost to you, as He did to Job?

Day 20: From Crushed Grapes to Fine Wine

Romans 8:18 (NLT) Yet what we suffer now is nothing compared to the glory he will reveal to us later.

A guy I knew worked in a fancy restaurant that sat on a lake. Most everyone who dined there came for the wine. The restaurant offered tons of choices, and their knowledge of wine was impeccable. They could tell you what wine paired best with what meat and what dessert tasted best with what wine. They had tableside wine service, opening the bottle and pulling the corks with grace, and single-handedly pouring a glass of wine without wasting a drop. Guests were not allowed to pour their own glasses. If they got to the wine to pour their own glass before the server could get there, it was considered bad service in the eyes of the owner.

Wine was highly regarded in that restaurant, and it made up the bulk of their sales. It is why people came and what the restaurant was known for. Yet that restaurant would not have had all of its success without the wine-making process. You will not have your success without going through the process. The obstacles and difficulties can feel like they are crushing you at times. There is no making wine without first crushing the grapes! When you feel like you are being crushed by life, just know that you are being pressed to success. You've heard of being dressed for success? Well, you are being pressed for success by your struggles!

I am sure that if you asked anyone you consider to be successful, their story of success would be one of struggle. It is almost like the two go hand in hand. The struggle is where you gain wisdom, strength, and make the changes needed to be successful in the life that God has called you to live.

Keep your eyes on the wine and not on the grapes. Think about the end glory that will be produced in you when the time of pressing is over. You have to be able to see past your present circumstances if you are going to stay encouraged.

Keeping yourself encouraged is one of the vital parts of making it through the struggle. Keeping your eyes ahead and off your current circumstances is a great way to do it.

I wonder if you were to be a fly on the wall in that restaurant if you would hear anyone talking about the grapes what were used in making the wine. "Oh, those poor grapes! I can't believe they crushed those grapes like that!" Or "Those grapes didn't do anything to anyone; they did not deserve that." No one thinks about the grapes' suffering; they are too busy enjoying what the grapes produced. They are not concerned with the hardship that the grapes endured. They are more interested in the great taste that came out of it.

You also should not be concerned with the smashing of grapes in your life because in the end you know the result will be a fine wine. That should be what you focus on. Think about how good the wine is going to taste when it is all over, how well it is going to go with your meal, and how all the crushing was worth it.

If you were to stand up close to a painting and only focus on one small area, you would have no idea what that painting was about. You probably would not even be able to make out what you are looking at. You must see the full picture if you are going to appreciate the beauty of the art.

So, try to look at the full picture in life instead of the small view of your current circumstances. Think about God's faithfulness and how you can be sure He is going to bring you out of your difficulties. Don't worry about the grapes. I promise when you taste the wine, the crushed grapes are not going to matter anymore.

In Mark 14:25 NIV, Jesus said, "Truly I tell you, I will not drink again from the fruit of the vine until that day when I drink it new in the kingdom of God."

Let's be ready to drink that wonderful new wine with Jesus. The vision of that can sustain us as we go through the pressing process on the way to the kingdom of God.

Questions for Consideration

1. When you are pressed, you may feel depressed, oppressed, stressed, and distressed. That is not what you really are, though. What word rhymes with the above and starts with a B? That's what you really are!

2. Do you know someone who has gone through tough times and come out better than ever before?

3. In Matthew 9:17 Jesus talked about pouring new wine into new wineskins. Do you believe you are being renewed in Jesus?

4. Can you see your struggles as part of the renewal process?

Day 21: Dealing With Rejection

Isaiah 53:3 (NLT) He was despised and rejected—
a man of sorrows, acquainted with deepest grief.
We turned our backs on him and looked the other way.
He was despised, and we did not care.

One of the things I enjoy doing is going to the mall and eating in the food court. I especially enjoy observing young people in their interactions with one another. It brings back so many memories for me of when I was younger.

There was a time not long ago when I felt like I was watching an episode of *National Geographic* where the male animal is trying to get the female animal's attention. One guy with a group of his friends was getting a pep talk to go and talk to a cute girl nearby. He even spent the last three minutes with his friends, thinking of the best line he could come up with: "There is no way you can be from around here because you are the finest girl I have ever seen." He finally worked up his nerve to go over to her. It was obvious it took everything in him to muster up that line, and he said it with as much confidence as he could.

The next part was the hard part: waiting to see what her response would be. He tried to pay attention to her facial expression while he was talking to find out whether he would be rejected or not, but he couldn't tell.

"Thank you but no thank you," she said as she and all her friends giggled. He was heartbroken and embarrassed. Still, the next time he tried he would not be so hurt by the rejection, and he would be more prepared.

Rejection can feel like a blow to the chest. If you get hit in the chest enough times, though, you will start to protect yourself. Rejection can be the blow that makes you stronger. It can make you fight harder rather than defeating you.

Jesus was rejected by the very people he was sent to save. Talk about rejection! Jesus suffered the ultimate rejection of being put to death. One man who transformed his life during prison once said that being sentenced to death by society was the ultimate form of rejection by that society. That is what the society of his time did to Jesus. Yet that rejection helped to fulfill the will of God.

What if they never rejected Jesus? What if everyone loved Jesus, and approved of what he was doing? He would not have been brought before the rulers if no one had complained about him. How would he have died for us if the people loved everything about him and didn't reject him?

Although hurtful, rejection can be exactly what we need to create inward determination. Rejection could be the very thing that pushes you to get focused and try harder. "I'll show them!" has motivated many a successful person.

An actress recently did an interview and talked about her journey to becoming successful. When she moved out to California to pursue her dreams, she was met by nothing but rejection after rejection. They gave her every excuse they could find as to why she wasn't right for parts. She was too short, not talented enough, and on and on. There was always some reason why, according to them, she did not meet their standards.

Most people would have given up at that point, but not her. She had a dream in her heart, and she was not going to let anyone convince her that it would not come true. Even her friends met her with rejection, telling her she was too old to be just starting her acting career.

All that rejection became the fuel to her fire; it made her try harder. Not only was she going to live her dream, but she was determined to prove that everyone who doubted her was wrong. Now she is seen everywhere as an actress. She is living out her dreams, like she always knew she would.

Have you been rejected? Were you turned for a job? Did someone break off a relationship with you? Were you rejected by a college? Has one of your family members cut off all communication? Rejection hurts, there is no doubt about that.

Yet don't let it get you down. Allow it to push you into greatness. Did the rejection upset you? Then redirect your anger and use it as fuel to make sure that you receive everything God has for you.

God in all of His wisdom used the rejection of others to accomplish the greatest plan of redemption that the world has ever seen. Don't take others' rejecting words to heart. Put them to work as a catapult to your dreams.

Questions for Consideration

1. Thinking of Jesus, can you see that even the most beautiful, perfect, and loving person might sometimes suffer rejection?

2. Can you refuse to take rejection personally?

3. Can you use it as a spur to better yourself next time?

4. What is the true measure of your worth—how others may see you or how God sees you?

Day 22: The Power of Resilience

Ephesians 6:13-14 (NLT)
Therefore, put on every piece of God's armor so you will be able to resist the enemy in the time of evil. Then after the battle you will still be standing firm. 14 Stand your ground, putting on the belt of truth and the body armor of God's righteousness.

When I was younger I used to love watching cartoons, I think all children did. The cartoons now are nowhere near as great as the ones we used to watch, but I may be a bit biased. Do you remember *Wiley Coyote*? Every single show would be about him trying to catch the Road Runner. Although the plot for the show never changed, that did not stop us from watching it. Some would call the coyote resilient, but I think the it was the Road Runner who was the resilient one.

The Road Runner was always under attack by the coyote, just as you are always under attack. Just like you the Road Runner always got away. There was the coyote, every episode, still trying to destroy the Road Runner. Every episode, the Road Runner escaped every attempt of the coyote to destroy him. The coyote didn't stand a chance, and neither do the obstacles in your life.

You have to be like the Road Runner and just keep moving. Don't sit down, don't give in to the circumstances. You have to continue to stand.

I love the focus verse for today! Have you already done everything you can do to stand firm? Stand anyway. I am sure the Road Runner probably got tired of running but he kept running anyway.

There have been times when I have gone through difficult circumstances, and I would call my friend in a plea for pity and say, "I am tiring of standing." He would always say, "Then stand some more." What other choice do you have? Failure, defeat, destruction?

None of those are options for you. You have God living inside of you, and defeat is not in His vocabulary. It should not be in yours.

Is the coyote going to leave you alone? No. Are trials and tribulations going to stop? Unfortunately, the answer to that question is also no.

Yet you don't need the struggles to stop. You simply need to see the struggles for what they are. They are nothing compared to the power of God. The coyote can come with all the dynamite and tricks he can find, but he will never be able to catch up with you. When you stay focused on God, you are always one step ahead of him.

Don't worry about the coyote and what he has planned for you next. He will always be planning something. You have to stay focused on pressing forward. You must keep running towards God's desires for you, no matter what things come your way. You are gaining strength, momentum, and speed. You are getting better with each stride. Keep running. Keep believing.

Be able to say, as Paul did in 2 Timothy 4:7: "I have fought the good fight; I have finished the race; I have kept the faith."

Questions for Consideration

1. Are trials, struggles, setbacks, and adversity going to stop coming in your life?

2. What is the alternative to standing firm?

3. What does the Road Runner symbolize?

4. As a parent, wouldn't you want your children to have this quality? Does God want any less for us?

Day 23: Patiently Enduring Every Trial

Romans 5:2-4 (NLT) Because of our faith, Christ has brought us into this place of undeserved privilege where we now stand, and we confidently and joyfully look forward to sharing God's glory. We can rejoice, too, when we run into problems and trials, for we know that they help us develop endurance. And endurance develops strength of character, and character strengthens our confident hope of salvation.

Patience is something a person never seems to have enough of. There is a limit to everyone's patience. One may be patient enough to stand in a line with five people in front but not patient enough to stand in a line with ten people ahead. One may be patient enough to sit in traffic for twenty minutes but not for forty-five. We could all use more patience in our lives. Even the most patient person could probably use a little more.

How do you obtain patience? Is it something that you just have or is it something that you need to work on? I know that we are not born with patience. If you have ever been around a hungry baby or one who needs a diaper change, you can agree that they were not born with patience. If patience is not something we are born with, then where can it come from? How do we get it?

I remember when I was young and anxious about things taking too long, my mom would say, "Be patient." That was always easier said than done!

Waiting because you don't have a choice is completely different from patience. If you are stuck in a long line and can't get out of it, just staying there does not mean that you have patience. If the whole time you are in line you complain, roll your eyes, and tap your feet in irritation, that is not patience.

When you are going through the storms of life, you have two choices. You can learn to be patient or you can be miserable while you wait. The choice is yours.

It is true that our struggles do not last forever. It is also true that you will need patience if you are going to endure. Going through the rough and tough times in life develops patience in us.

How does the testing of our faith produce patience in us? Because when our faith is tested, it forces us to be patient or at least to learn how to be patient. Patience and trust go hand in when you are going through storms with God by your side.

Have you ever been an impatient driver or witnessed an impatient driver in traffic? You watch them dip in and out of lanes, speeding up and slowing down, doing whatever they have to do to make them feel like they are going somewhere when in all reality in just a moment you will be pulling up beside them again.

Being impatient does not help anything. It does not help you to get out of the storm faster, but it does make the time you spend in the storm worse. When you are patient in the trials of life, it is because you trust that God is working on your behalf. There is no need to be up in arms about the time it is taking for things to come together or turn around for you. God will not fail you, and His timing is perfect. When you develop the kind of patience that is established in trust, you are able to endure the storm joyfully and in peace.

The clouds may be dark but peeking through the clouds, you can see the sun. There is hope; you can see your storm is not going to last forever. If you look close enough into your situation, you will see the son. He is there creating a clear path, so you can leave those days of trouble behind. When you have hope in your heart, patience is sure to follow.

As John Quincy Adams said, "Patience and perseverance have a magical effect before which difficulties disappear and obstacles vanish."

When you know that God is coming to rescue you, it becomes easier to wait. Don't become restless during the tough times. Put your trust in God and wait patiently as He works to free you from the things that are trying to keep you bound. You will indeed see your difficulties disappear and your obstacles vanish.

Questions for Consideration

1. Can you eliminate such thinking as "Things shouldn't be this way for me" or "This isn't the way things are supposed to be"? They only lead to impatience.

2. Have you ever waited a long time for something or someone wonderful to come to you or to return to you? Was it worth the wait?

3. Do you have confidence that God has perfect timing and you should go with His flow?

Day 24: His Grace Is All You Need

2 Corinthians 12:8-9 (NLT) Three different times I begged the Lord to take it away. 9 Each time he said, "My grace is all you need. My power works best in weakness." So now I am glad to boast about my weaknesses, so that the power of Christ can work through me.

Have you ever felt like you were under attack? Have you ever felt like there was a force constantly working against you, creating suffering in your life? If the answer is yes, then you have a lot in common with the rest of the world.

You also have something in common with Paul. Paul was a man who was used mightily by God. He went from persecuting Christians to having a ministry of bringing the Gospel to the gentiles.

Paul was full of revelatory knowledge. In other words, God revealed many things to him. Because of this, Satan sent a messenger to harass Paul. Does that sound familiar to you? Do you feel like you are being harassed by the problems in your life?

I know there have been times in my life where everything that could go wrong, did. It was almost like a line of dominoes someone decided to tip over, with every piece falling, one by one.

Have you ever been around a gnat? Gnats must be one of the most annoying insects I have ever encountered. They fly around in your face, they buzz in your ear, and they try to get your food. Gnats are relentless! That is what the harassment of problems in your life can feel like: annoying gnats. You just want to yell from the top of your lungs, "Leave me alone!" If I am being honest, I have to admit I have yelled that before.

Paul probably felt that way too. Instead of yelling, though, Paul called upon the Lord three times.

Anyone would probably look at what Paul did and think he did the right thing. He went straight to Jesus and asked for his help. That is what we are supposed to do, right? What else is there to do to stop the harassment? Jesus had an answer for Paul, and he has the same answer for you:"My grace is all you need."

What kind of answer is that? This man was being harassed by Satan and all Jesus had to say was: "My grace is sufficient for you." If you are reading the same Scripture I am reading, that seems anything but sufficient. Then there was: "My strength is perfect in weakness." Great. Paul was really going through adversity and here was Jesus trying to give him a positive word of encouragement. Paul didn't need a positive word, though. He needed results. He needed someone to make something happen for him.

Yet that was precisely what God was saying. He was telling Paul that His grace and His strength was all that he needed to combat the harassment of the enemy. Paul knew that, though. This was not Paul's first rodeo. This was a man who walked in the power and authority of God. He knew what Jesus was saying was true. Sometimes, though, we don't want to stir ourselves up to stand against Satan.

The Bible says resist Satan and he will flee. That is all Paul had to do, but he simply didn't want to.

Have you ever been sick and just wanted to lie in the bed.? I'm sure we have all had days when all we wanted to do was pull the cover up over our heads and make the bed our permanent place of residence for the next three to four days. Yet I think almost everyone knows that you feel better when you get out of the bed.

I used to get so frustrated because as long as I was lying down, my nose would get stopped up, but the moment I would get up, it would clear. I would feel so much better when I was up and doing things. When it came time to go to bed, all the symptoms would come rushing in. But laying down feels good. It lets us wallow in self-pity.

Sometimes we just want someone to feel sorry for us and pity us. We would love to have someone tend to our needs, bring us tissues, soup, and cough medicine instead of getting out of the bed.

God was not going to let Paul do that, though. Instead of giving into Paul's desire, He reminded him that he had everything he needed to get rid of the messenger of Satan.

You also have everything you need. God knew good and well what Paul needed.

Satan also came harassing Jesus when he was fasting in the wilderness. Jesus could have easily gone crying to God, begging Him to make Satan leave him alone. But instead he resisted Satan with the Word of God. Then Satan left.

You must get up and fight. Don't just lie down and allow the enemy to walk all over you. You have the grace and strength of Christ. When you resist the devil, according to God's Word, he must flee. Make him do so. Then stride forward toward your success.

Questions for Consideration

1. Have you ever wanted to hide in bed for a few days?

2. Were you in a state of self-pity, wanting someone to feel sorry for you and help you?

3. How did you cope with the situation?

4. If you've picked up and gone on before, is there any reason why you can't do it again now?

Day 25: Surviving Life's Storms—Learning From The Three Little Pigs

Matthew 7:24-27 (NLT) 24 Anyone who listens to my teaching and follows it is wise, like a person who builds a house on solid rock. 25 Though the rain comes in torrents and the floodwaters rise and the winds beat against that house, it won't collapse because it is built on bedrock. 26 But anyone who hears my teaching and doesn't obey it is foolish, like a person who builds a house on sand. 27 When the rains and floods come and the winds beat against that house, it will collapse with a mighty crash.

When you are building something, you always want to make sure the foundation is strong. It does not matter if you are building a house, a car, or a business; the foundation needs to be able to stand the tests of time. You can only go on for so long with a foundation that is not solid, before everything begins to fall apart. We have all seen people's life destroyed for a lack of a strong foundation.

I know that everyone knows the story of the three little pigs. To a child the story doesn't mean much more than entertainment. As I sit here, though, I find that story is filled with much more truth than I ever realized. Just in case you forgot the story, let's review it.

There were three little pigs, and all three of these pigs had a house. Their houses were all built out of different materials. One was made with straw, another with sticks, and the last one with bricks.

There came a big bad wolf who wanted nothing else but to devour the pigs. There is a wolf in your life who is also looking to devour and destroy whatever he can get his hands on.

The wolf stopped at the first house, and I am sure you know what happened next. He huffed, and he puffed, and he blew the straw house down. Then he came the second house. It was made of different material, but the result was the same. The wolf huffed and puffed and blew down the second pig's house. Surely the third pig's house would be no match for the mighty wind of the wolf.

The wolf huffed and puffed but the house of the third pig would not fall. He huffed and puffed again, but still the house would not budge. The house of the third pig was built with a strong foundation. The wolf could have stayed out there huffing and puffing all day and night, but that house would not have fallen.

Your enemies can also try with all their might to tear down your house, your reputation, your marriage, and your business, but they cannot prevail if you are standing on a sure foundation.

What is this foundation that can stand against that attacks of the enemy? It is being obedient to the word of God. It is being a doer and not a hearer only.

You see, when you are only a hearer of the Word, the Bible says you are not standing on a strong foundation. It is in the doing of the Word that faith and trust are established. You love God and believe His Word is true when you are a doer of the word.

The Scripture doesn't say that winds are not going to come, and rains are not going to fall just because you built your house on a strong foundation. It says only that your house will stand against the tribulations.

When you are a doer, you trust in His guidance; you are sure of His faithfulness towards you, and thus you are unmoved by the storms of life. Doers of the Word don't run for cover when it begins to rain.

They stand with their feet planted, their backs straight, and their heads held high, because they have an umbrella they know will protect them. The Word of God is our umbrella. The umbrella cannot promise you that it will not rain, but it can promise you that you won't get wet.

The Bible says that we will have troubles. If we live on this earth, there will be difficulties that we have to endure. Yet we were made to be conquerors through the Word of God.

I have been going to church for a long time, and it is easy to spot someone who is only a hearer of the Word. It is someone who goes to church but doesn't do anything with what they have learned. It was a great sermon and may have even been exactly what they needed, but when they don't become a doer, those words falls away.

I used to wonder how is that people can spend years in church and still be the same, as if they never got saved. It is because they are hearers of the Word only.

Hearing the word is like putting your car key in the ignition, but being a doer of the Word is starting the car. Putting the key in the ignition is great, but if you want to get somewhere, you will have to rev up the engine.

Being a hearer of the Word will only get you so far. The minute there is an attack on your life you have no defenses. Without acting on the Word, you are as helpless as a newborn baby.

I can tell you how to get to my house, but unless you go, you are never going to arrive. You will not be able to magically show up at my house because you heard me give you directions. You must do what you heard me say.

I encourage you to be more than a hearer. To build your life on a sure foundation, begin by being a doer of the Word.

Questions for Consideration

1. What does it mean to be a hearer of the Word?

2. What does it mean to be a doer of the Word?

3. What are some examples of being a doer of the Word?

4. Are you more of a hearer or a doer of the Word?

Day 26: Process ... Process ... Process

Jeremiah 29:11 (NLT) For I know the plans I have for you, says the Lord. They are plans for good and not for disaster, to give you a future and a hope.

I love a good roast; it's a good hearty meal perfect for the fall. To me the best way to eat a roast is with carrots and potatoes. Who can turn down a tender roast that is falling apart on the fork? The longer you cook a roast the better the results will be, the more tender it will turn out. The more tender the roast, the better.

There is no rushing the cooking of a roast. It is meant to be cooked on low heat for a long period of time. If you tried to rush the process by turning up the heat and leaving it in the oven for a shorter amount of time. you would end up with an overcooked, tough, chewy roast. Who wants that?

That is how many of us live our lives. We want to rush the process. We want to speed everything up, hurry up and get it over with.

How can you try to speed up something that is meant for your good, meant for perfecting and preparing you for the next phase of your life? Life is full of processes. When you try to skip and rush them, something will always go wrong.

I know a woman who put a straightener in her hair. She wanted to bypass the process and the time it takes, so she bought a stronger one because it would work faster. It worked faster all right. In about a week's time, her hair was falling out and she had a bald spot in the back of her head.

Have you ever stopped to ask yourself: What is the rush? Why do you have to push through the process so fast? Do you feel like life is going to move forward without you? Do you think you are going to miss something important? You won't. The most important thing you need to worry about missing is the preparation God is trying to take you through. You can miss that by rushing.

God knows exactly what we need and how long it takes to develop things in us. What if God brought you to the next level of your life before you were ready? Do you know what would happen? You would fail. Or even worse, you would destroy yourself.

We see celebrities all the time who are thrust into the spot light and they are not ready for it. The temptations and pleasures of that kind of life overwhelm them. The next thing you know, they are checking into rehab, are in and out of jail, canceling shows, or committing suicide. God loves us too much to bring us into the life that He has prepared for us prematurely. It is hard for many people to see it as love because they don't understand the heart of God, nor can they see what He sees. We have a limited view of what is in store for us. God has a full view of our future, He knows everything He has planned for us.

The key to enduring the process is in knowing that God's plans for you are good. See your detours and adversities in life as preparation. See them as time taken chopping up the potatoes and carrots and getting the roast ready to bake. We have to learn to be like a roast, to allow God to take the time necessary to perfect us so He can take us to the next stop on our journey.

Our lives will be full of processes, so we might as well get used to it. The thing about God is, He will continually take you to a greater and deeper place in Him but that will mean more time in the oven, more cooking, more perfecting.

If you want everything God has for you, if you want to live out the life that He has planned for you, then you must be open to the process.

The more you take from the process, the more you learn from it, and the more you allow it to make you better. In that way you will be all the greater at your next stop.

Questions for Consideration

1. Have you ever skipped some steps to a process and found out your project was ruined because of it?

2. How does going through the proper process relate to what was said earlier about patience?

3. Have you ever turned in a project that was only partially completed and been rejected because of that?

Day 27: Keep Digging For Gold

Proverbs 16:16 (NLT) How much better to get wisdom than gold, and good judgment than silver!

Everyone loves gold. They wear it around their necks, on their fingers, around their wrists, and in their ears. Even if you are not a fan of gold, who wouldn't mind getting their hands on some to cash in?

Gold is easily accessible. You can probably go to your nearest store and find several pieces of gold jewelry. If you were to find it for yourself, though, you would have to dig.

God's plan and promises are like gold. If we are being honest, we know they are better than gold.

The word of God is the shovel used to obtain promises. When you come to roadblocks in your life, that is the perfect opportunity to start digging for gold.

The Word of God is filled with promises for every situation you may face. The only way you're going to find them, though, is by looking for them. There are no excuses in our days of technology why you cannot find what you are looking for. Back in the day you would have to search the Scriptures for yourself or rely on the Concordance in the back of your Bible for help. These days you have Google, and it is as simple as typing in "Scriptures about finances," or "Scriptures about health," or "Scriptures about marriage." Whatever the need is, I can guarantee you that God has a Scripture that will see you through.

Every time you meditate on His Scripture for the adversity in your life, you are digging deeper. The more attention you give the Word, the deeper you dig and the closer you are to the gold. Don't give up!

There was a man who went digging for gold. He had all his tools, even his helmet with a headlight. He was sure today was the day he was going to find some gold.

When he first started digging, he was full of excitement. He was moving fast and full of energy. The longer he kept digging, the slower he got and the less excited he became.He wanted to give up, but he kept digging, knowing there had to be gold somewhere. Soon the desire to quit was greater than his desire for gold.

He began to doubt: "What if there never was gold here? It was dumb of me to think I could find some." Before he knew it, he felt defeated and with that defeat he gave up. He stopped digging. He gathered his equipment and started to leave.

A little boy had been watching. The boy wondered what the man was looking for. In his curiosity, he started to dig where the man left off.

Looking back, the man shook his head.

"You're not going to find anything in there, kid," he yelled.

But by the time the man got to the top of the hill, he heard the boy scream: "Mom, mom, I found gold."

The man's heart was broken. If he only would have tried a little longer that would have been his gold.

Many of you have been struggling for a long time. You have been holding on to your Scriptures for what seems like no avail. Just like the man in the story, you have been digging and digging, and now you feel you can't dig any more. Your arms are sore, and you are covered in dirt.

Let me assure you, this is not the time to give up. You have been struggling for too long now to get tired in well doing. The more you dig the closer you are getting. It could be only one more dig away.

Are you tired? Is the dirt of struggles covering your life? Then now is the time to grip the shovel with all your might and dig for the gold that you have already been so diligently working to receive.

The Bible verse at the beginning says the wisdom of God is better than gold. His wisdom is found in his Word. Many would probably hold gold at a higher value than the Word of God, but His words are priceless.

So, keep digging. Keep standing on the Word of God for your circumstances. Before you know it, you will find your gold.

Questions for Consideration

1. Recall a time when you wanted to give up but did not. What helped you go on?

2. What might have happened if the little boy had encouraged the man? After all, Sonia Gandhi said, "Together we can face any challenges as deep as the ocean and as high as the sky."

3. Do you sometimes find gold in the words of encouragement you find in the Bible or from kindly others?

Day 28: Commitment—Staying the Course

1 Corinthians 2:2 (NLT) For I decided that while I was with you I would forget everything except Jesus Christ, the one who was crucified.

Not many people know the meaning of commitment today. Marriages are failing left and right. People can hardly make a commitment to their jobs anymore, let alone a relationship.

Is commitment just a pastime that will someday cease to exist? I don't believe so, because we serve a God of commitment. If there are people who are wholeheartedly serving Him, there will always be people who are serious about commitment because God is serious about commitment.

The marriages that last are among those who have decided that they are going to be committed to each other no matter what. That is, after all, what the vows say! Talk of divorce is never an option for committed people. Calling it quits was never in the plan. Commitment is not about feelings, because feelings are easily swayed and changed. We know that our feelings can be affected by a rainy or sunny day! When it comes to marriage, our feelings are no barometer of commitment, because feelings come, go, and transform over time. Instead, commitment is about making a decision and sticking to it, no matter what happens.

Paul was a man who had committed his life to Christ and that life of commitment was obvious to anyone who saw it.

When Paul determined to forget everything else, as the verse says above, he was making a commitment to the Gospel and its truth. He was committed to live his life according to that and nothing else.

Do you think his commitment meant that Paul did not struggle? Commitment is often followed by trials. Paul's commitment landed him in jail repeatedly, and it made him a target of those wanting to silence the Gospel.

That is the way commitment works. There is no plan B, no other choice or option. Struggles will come but that should not change your commitment. If anything, it should make it greater.

There will be struggles and hard times in marriage. There will be fights, disagreements, schedule conflicts, and financial setbacks. If there are children, the list could go on forever. Commitment is about giving it everything you got, in good times and bad.

It is easy to be committed when everything is going well. It is easy to persevere when your husband or wife is doing everything perfectly and your stomach is filled with butterflies of joy at the mere sight of him or her. But what about when your spouse messes up? What if he or she made a bad decision that affected you both or your whole family? What if one spouse did something that hurt the other? When the times get tough, that is when true commitment kicks in. You don't have a successful marriage without effort; you have one because you decided to be committed against all odds.

Times may be tough in your life. Tough times require committing yourself to stand on the Word of God and not settle for defeat, especially by a foe who has already been defeated. We do not overcome the things that happen in our life by accident. It is happening for a reason.

Do you have what it takes to stand on the Word of God in good times and bad? As a born-again Christian, you absolutely do. You have everything you need on the inside of to overcome anything on the outside.

The only reason we think that we cannot overcome is because we are looking at ourselves and our own abilities. As long as you are looking at yourself. You are right; you will never have what it takes. It is only through God that we able to prevail.

When Paul made a commitment, it was one that was founded on Christ. That is the best type of commitment to make. It is one you can be sure will produce results.

The next time you find yourself struggling, make a commitment to yourself and to God that you will stand on His Word without wavering. Commit yourself to not giving up and keeping your focus on Him.

We commit to things that we want to every day; we commit to go to the gym, to remember and check our phones, to watch the television shows we like at the times they come on. We are also very committed to our bad habits!

It is time that we commit to something greater. That commitment has the ability to change our setbacks into set-ups for success. It is as was said by the Dalai Lama: "When we meet real tragedy in life, we can react in two ways: either by losing hope and falling into self-destructive habits, or by using the challenge to find our inner strength." When challenges strike, that is time to call on our inner commitment to see us through.

Questions for Consideration

1. What commitments have you honored in your life, even when the going got tough?

2. Statistics say that people who said they were unhappy in their marriages became happier a few years later, after sticking to their wedding vows. What does this say about commitment?

3. What evidence do you see in your life of God's commitment to you?

Day 29: The Making of Pearls

Ecclesiastes 3:11(NLT)
Yet God has made everything beautiful for its own time.

I have a friend named July who shared a story with me concerning her and her little brother. When they were little kids, their mother would often take them to a popular lake near where they lived. One particular day the lake was full of people swimming, kayaking, and just enjoying themselves.

There was a part of the lake that will filled with rocks, and water was running over them. That is where July and her brother decided to play. Their mom obliged their request and took them over to the rocks. They both played in the water while sitting down on the rocks, watching the water rush over their legs. The water was warm, and they had the best seats to watch the families out on their boats.

July told me that when she got up from sitting down on the rocks, she felt something stuck to her legs. She looked down, and there were leeches all over her legs. She never felt them while she was sitting down. They had crept up on her unexpectedly when she was minding her own business.

Can you imagine the screaming and rushing to get the leeches off? They were definitely an unpleasant surprise!

That is exactly how trials and tribulations are. They will creep up on you when you least expect it. When you are busy living your life, they will sneak up on you unaware and try to suck your life dry, like a parasite. Out of this comes struggles and setbacks that strike you by surprise. They take the beauty that was in your life and try to turn it into something ugly and painful.

The struggles in our lives are like parasites that we must refuse to let weaken us. We can learn something about this from the pearl.

When a parasite makes its way into an oyster, the oyster defends itself by covering the parasite in a fluid. Then the oyster covers the parasite with layer after layer after layer of the fluid. Those layers of fluid become a pearl. In that way, something that was meant for harm was used to make something beautiful.

That's what God does with the struggles that come in our lives, the ones that aim to cause us harm and destruction. When you become overwhelmed with life's problems, you have your own defense mechanism. It is the word of God. Just as the pearl covers the parasite in layers of fluid, you are going to cover your obstacles with layer after layer of the Word of God and with prayer. The storms of life are no match for this. They never have been, and they never will be. Like the oyster, you will weave something beautiful and valuable over that life-sucking parasite that came into your life.

If there was no parasite, there would be no pearl. God is making precious pearls out of your struggles. There isn't one thing in our life that God can't take and turn into something beautiful. As long as we are willing to give it to Him, He will take it and transform it.

We have a tendency to hold on to the tough times we go through in life. We almost identify ourselves with them and make them our own! Yet our circumstances are not meant to be accepted; they are meant to be overcome.

Don't just let the parasite come and rob you of your life. Crush him with the weight of the Word, layer him over and over with prayer and watch God turn your struggles into pearls.

Questions for Consideration

1. Think of one of the greater hardships of your life. What pearls of faith emerged from it?

2. What did you learn about yourself?

3. What did you learn about God?

Day 30: Rubber Bands in His Hands

1 Peter 5:10 (NLT) In his kindness God called you to share in his eternal glory by means of Christ Jesus. So after you have suffered a little while, he will restore, support, and strengthen you, and he will place you on a firm foundation.

Rubber bands are such a simple invention, but they can be used for so many things! You can use one to put your hair up in a pony tail, to keep money together, or, if you were the little boy in my class, to flick and snap at people.

Rubber bands are great until you get popped by one. That hurts!

How can something so flimsy hurt so bad? It's the tension. The more you hold it back, the farther it goes and the harder it hits.

There will always be things in life that try to hold you back, creating tension. These things will try to stop you from going forward.

When adversity comes into your life, it seems like everything stops. Everything becomes focused on resisting the tension that the adversity has brought about. It seems like you can't move forward. The struggles in your life are holding you back.

Yet you don't have to allow those trials to be setbacks in your life. Instead you can use them like the tension on the rubber band to propel you forward into the things of God.

Stop looking at your struggles as something horrible. See them as the needed force to get you to your destination.

Most people know the story of the two fish and the five loaves in the New Testament. There was a group of people who had been following

Jesus. They had been following him for days. Jesus looked and saw the multitude and knew they needed to eat. He and his followers didn't have enough money to feed them all.

I am sure to the disciples this situation seemed a bit stressful. They didn't have enough money or resources to feed the multitude. In fact, in the biblical account, you can sense the worry and tension they felt (Matthew 14: 15-17 NIV):

15. As evening approached, the disciples came to him and said, "This is a remote place, and it's already getting late. Send the crowds away, so they can go to the villages and buy themselves some food."

16. Jesus replied, "They do not need to go away. You give them something to eat."

17. "We have here only five loaves of bread and two fish," they answered.

Jesus did not let the situation stress him, not even for a second. Instead, he saw a miracle in the making. As it turned out, once he had given thanks and broken the bread, he instructed the disciples to start passing out the food. Not only did they have enough to feed the multitude, there was food left over after everyone was done eating—twelve basket fulls of leftovers!.

Your situation may be looking a lot like theirs. Maybe you are short on money, out of resources, and what you have doesn't seem to be enough. We have the same options Jesus had. We can throw in the towel and decide we do not have what it takes, or we can expect the miraculous.

One of the best things I like about this story is that, instead of feeling overwhelmed, Jesus took the food and gave thanks. He took the very thing that seemed like it wasn't enough and blessed it. We too can give thanks for adversity, because, as Malcolm X said, "There is no better [teacher] than adversity. Every defeat, every heartbreak, every loss, contains its own seed, its own lesson on how to improve your performance the next time."

When you start to see the blessing in your trials, it is like pulling back a rubber band. When you go through things and start looking past the surface into what God is doing through your circumstances, you are creating the force needed to get you through. When you don't let setbacks define you but instead see the blessing lying beneath, you will soon be thrust into all God has for you. The struggles will be the tension you need to spring forward with force, just like the rubber band.

Questions for Consideration

1. Have you ever given thanks for what you had, even though it didn't seem to be enough?

2. Did you experience the miracle of multiplication?

3. Did you know that scientists have found that giving thanks is an antidote to depression and feeling down about life?

Day 31: You've Got a Friend in Me

John 15:13 (NLT) There is no greater love than to lay down one's life for one's friends.

I don't know if you have ever seen the movie *Toy Story*, but if you haven't, you should, no matter what age you are. *Toy Story* is just as it sounds; it follows the story of some toys who belong to a boy named Andy. There are several *Toy Story* movies that follow the toys as they face the every day challenges of being the toys of a kid who is growing up. Every movie offers a new challenge and a new victory. Friends are lost along the way, changes are made, and lives are impacted, but the movies never end without victory.

The main character in the story is Woody. He is a toy cowboy with a positive attitude who does not know when to give up. Then you have Buzz Lightyear, his best friend, who is always anxious to help.

I watched this movie recently, and I couldn't help but think about God. There is no better friend than God. As with Buzz Lightyear, it does not always seem like He is going to come through, but He is always there just in time, whenever we need Him.

It also made me think about how we should be more like Woody when faced with challenges in life. Woody faces anything that comes his way head on, making a plan of action and fearlessly aiming for victory.

Also, Woody and Buzz went through everything together: jealousy, misunderstandings, getting lost in life, and being mistreated. No matter what they went through, they did it together. We often go through our trials alone. We don't want anyone to know what we are going through. Maybe we are even ashamed of the decisions or actions that got us into our difficulties. Yet God doesn't care about any of that. He just loves you and wants to be the friend you need during your hard times.

God is the type of friend who will never let you down and will always be there for you. Some of the roughest times in my life were just me and God. I had no one to confide in, no one whose advice I trusted. There was no one I could entrust with what I was going through. Yet there was Jesus with his open arms and ears, waiting to listen to everything I had to say. He let me pour out my heart until there wasn't a drop left. After letting me vent, he would always comfort me and help me to press past anything I was going through.

I think the problem is many people do not see Jesus as a friend. They do not see him as someone they can talk to or confide in.

"You've Got a Friend in Me" is one of my favorite songs. It's from the first *Toy Story* movie. Its words are a perfect picture of our friendship with God: "You've got a friend in me, you've got a friend in me. When the road looks rough ahead and you're miles and miles from your nice warm bed, just remember what your old pal said: 'Boy, you've got a friend in me.' And as the years go by, our friendship will never die. You're gonna see, it's our destiny. You've got a friend in me."

I can't hear or sing that song anymore without thinking about Jesus. After going through so many things with him right by my side, he has proven himself to be a friend indeed. If you see him as the friend he is, you won't have to go through your adversities alone. Take the load of life off your back and give it over to Jesus. Let him carry it like the good and loving friend that he is.

It is often not enough just to call someone your friend. Giving someone the title of "friend" does not qualify that person for the role. Friendship is tried and tested, and true friendship lasts in the midst of it all.

Jesus' friendship already stood the test of time when he died for us, when he gave up his life for all his friends. That's what he said he was doing, and that was what he called all his followers: friends.

Never forget that you can always trust God to be the truest friend there is. He will love you regardless of what you are going through. Lean on Him and let His friendship be the love you need during your trying times.

Questions for Consideration

1. Have you ever been so alone in a struggle that you had no one to turn to but God?

2. How did that particular struggle turn out?

3. Do you believe God is the best friend you will ever have?

4. What in your life has demonstrated this?

Made in the USA
Columbia, SC
11 June 2018